Augustus Montague Toplady

The Scheme of Christian and philosophical necessity asserted

With a Dissertation concerning the sensible Qualities of Matter

Augustus Montague Toplady

The Scheme of Christian and philosophical necessity asserted
With a Dissertation concerning the sensible Qualities of Matter

ISBN/EAN: 9783337242275

Printed in Europe, USA, Canada, Australia, Japan

Cover: Foto ©ninafisch / pixelio.de

More available books at **www.hansebooks.com**

SCHEME

OF

CHRISTIAN AND PHILOSOPHICAL

NECESSITY

ASSERTED.

In Opposition to Mr. *John Wesley*'s Tract on that Subject.

WITH A

DISSERTATION

CONCERNING THE

SENSIBLE QUALITYS

OF

MATTER:

AND THE

DOCTRINE OF COLOR IN PARTICULAR.

By AUGUSTUS TOPLADY,
VICAR OF BROAD HEMBURY.

" Adeò stat et permanet invicta Sententia, *Omnia* NECESSITATE *fieri.* Nec est hîc ulla Obscuritas, aut Ambiguitas. In Esaiâ dicit [Deus], *Consilium Meum stabit, et Voluntas Mea fiet.* Quis enim Puer non intelligit quid velint hæc Vocabula, *Consilium, Voluntas, fiet, stabit?*" LUTHER. de Servo Arbitrio, Sect. 19.

" Quæ nobis videtur Contingentia, *secretum* DEI *Impulsum* fuisse agnoscet Fides." CALVIN. Institut. L. 1. C. 16.

" Quid igitur, inquies, Nullane est in Rebus, ut istorum Vocabulo utar, Contingentia? Nihil Casus? Nihil Fortuna?—*Omnia* NECESSARIÒ *evenire* Scripturæ docent." MELANCTHON. Loc. Com. P. 10. Edit. *Argentor.* 1523.

" There is not a FLY, but has had INFINITE WISDOM *concerned, not only in it's* STRUCTURE, *but in it's* DESTINATION." Dr. Young's Cent. not fab. Letter II.

LONDON:
Printed for VALLANCE and SIMMONS in CHEAPSIDE.
M.DCC.LXXV.

CONTENTS.

*P*REFACE   Page i.

CHAPTER I.

Necessity defined. — Short Account of Fate, and the Order observed in the Chain of Things. — Necessity perfectly compatible with Voluntary Freedom.

                                             P. 9.

CHAPTER II.

Man a compound Being. — Sensation the only Source of his Ideas. — The Soul's extensive Dependence on the Body, during their present State of Connection. — An Argument, drawn from thence, for the

the Neceſſity of Human Volitions. — Quærys, propoſed to the Aſſertors of Self-Determination.
Page 18.

CHAPTER III.

Probable Equality of Human Souls. — Brutes themſelves not merely Material. — Neceſſity conſiſtent with the Morality of Actions : — and with Reward and Puniſhment, Praiſe and Blame : — and with the Retributions of the Judgement Day. — No Certainty, nor Poſſibility, of a final Judgement, on the Arminian Principles of Chance and Self-Determination. — Anti-Neceſſitarians unable to cope with Infidels. — Co-incidence of Chriſtian Predeſtination with Philoſophical Neceſſity.
P. 33.

CHAPTER IV.

Specimen of Scripture-Atteſtations to the Doctrine of Neceſſity. — Probable, that Men are, by Nature, uncivilized Animals. — Total Dependency of All Events, and of All Created Beings, on God. P. 56.

CHAPTER

CONTENTS.

CHAPTER V.

Proofs that CHRIST Himself was an absolute Necessitarian. — This argued from several Passages in His Sermon on the Mount: — from His Miracles: — from His Fore-knowledge: — from His Prophecys: — from His occasional Declarations: — and from the whole History of His Life and Death recorded in the Gospels.   Page 71.

CHAPTER VI.

Necessity, in the Moral World; analogous to Attraction, in the Natural. — Prodigious Length, to which Des Cartes is said to have carryed his Idea of Free-will. — Mors, and Fatum, why reciprocated by the antient Romans. — God the sole Determiner of Human Life and Death. — Shocking Attempts of some modern Free-willers to divest the Divine Being, not only of His Decrees and Providence, but of His Præscience also.   P. 98.

CHAPTER VII.

The supposed Gloominess of Necessity, refuted. — Origin of Doctrinal Necessity. — Concise History,

and

CONTENTS.

and Summary, of Manichæism. — *Methodists more gross Manichæans, than Manes himself.* — *Remarkable Conversation-Pieces of Three modern Philosophizers.* — *The* Westminster *and other Assemblys of Divines, vindicated.* — *Arminianism itself, when hard pushed, compel'd to take Refuge in Necessity.* — CONCLUSION *of this Essay.*

Page 119.

APPENDIX.

Consisting of a DISSERTATION *on the* SENSIBLE QUALITYS *of Matter.* P. 163—205.

PREFACE.

PREFACE.

YESTERDAY's Poſt brought me a Packet from London, including, among other Papers, a ſmall Tract, recently publiſhed by Mr. *John Weſley*, entitled, "Thoughts upon "Neceſſity." I had no ſooner peruſed thoſe "Thoughts," than I reſolved to bring them to the Teſt: and am now ſetting about it.

During ſome Years paſt, I have, for the moſt part, ſtood patiently on *the Defenſive*, againſt this Gentleman. 'Tis high Time, that I take *my* Turn to INVADE; and carry the Arms of Truth into the Enemy's own Territory.

Mr. Weſley's Tract, above-mentioned, was ſent to me, by a well-known, and very deſerving, London Clergyman. So much of whoſe Letter,

[ii]

as relates to the said Tract, shall, for the Amusement of my Readers, be submitted to their View.

"I went, last Night, to the * Foundery; expecting to hear Pope *John*: but was disappointed. After hearing a Welshman, for an Hour and twenty Minutes, on Psalm lxxxiv. 11. preach up all the Heresys of the Place; a Man, who sat in the Pulpit, told him to 'Give over': For he seemed to bid fair for another Half Hour, at least. But he came to a Conclusion, as desired. Then this Man, who seemed to be a local Preacher, stood up, with a Pamphlet in his Hand, and addressed the Auditory in the following Manner:

'*I am desired, to publish a Pamphlet upon* NECESSITY *and* FREE-WILL; *the best extant, that I know of, in the* † English *Tongue: by Mr.* John Wesley, *Price* THREE-PENCE.—*I had purposed to have said a* GOOD DEAL *upon it: but the* TIME *is elapsed.*—*But, in this three-penny Pamphlet, you have* ALL *the Disputes that have been bandy'd about so lately. And you will get your Minds more*

---

* Mr. Wesley's principal Meeting-house in London.

† Query: Does the said Lay Preacher, whoever he may be, know aught of any *other* Tongue?

established

' *eſtabliſhed*, by THIS THREE-PENNY *Pamphlet*,
' *than by reading* ALL *the Books that have been*
' *written for and againſt.* It is to be had, at both
' Doors, *as You go out*.
  " I beg Leave" (adds my Reverend Friend),
" to tranſmit you this here ſaid ſame three-penny
" Wonder."

Upon the Whole, this muſt have been a droll Sort of Mountebank Scene. Attended, however, with one moſt melancholy and deplorable Circumſtance, ariſing from the unreaſonable and unſeaſonable Prolixity of the long-winded Holderforth: which cruelly, injudiciouſly, and deſpitefully, prevented poor *Zany* from puffing off, with the Amplitude he fully intended, the multiplex Virtues of the DOCTOR's three-penny freewill Powder.

Never do That by Delegation, ſays an old Proverb, *which you can as well do in propriâ Perſonâ*. Had Doctor JOHN himſelf got upon the Stage, and ſung,

  " Come, buy my fine Powders; come buy dem
     " of Me;
  " Hare be de beſt Powders dat ever you ſee:"

Who

Who knows, but the three-penny Doses might have gone off, "*at both Doors,*" as rapidly as Peas from a Pop-gun?

My Business, for a few spare Hours, shall be, to amuse myself, by *analysing* this redoubtable Powder. The chemical Resolution of so inestimable a Specific into its component Parts (a Specific,

"*The like whereto was never seen,*
"*Nor will again, while Grass is green*"),

may, moreover, be of very great and signal USE. 'Twere Pity, that the *Materia medica*, of which it is made up, should remain a Secret. Especially, as the good Doctor designed it for *general Benefit*. To make which Benefit as *universal* as I can, I do hereby give Notice, unto all Philosophers, Divines, and others, who have poison'd their Intrails, by unwarily taking too deep a Draught of NECESSITY; that they may, at any Time, by Help of the following Decomposition, have it in their Power to mix up, for their own immediate Recovery, a competent Quantum of the famous *Moor-fields Powder*: whose chief Ingredients are,

An equal Portion of gross *Heathenism, Pelagianism, Mahometism, Popery, Manichæism, Ranterism, rifm*, and *Antinomianifm*; cull'd, dryed, and pulveriz'd, *fecundum Artem*: and, above all, mingled with as much palpable *Atheifm* as you can poffibly fcrape together from every Quarter.

Hæ tibi erunt Artes. Follow the above Præfcription, to your Life's End; and you'll find it a moft pleafant, fpeedy, and infallible Antidote againft every Species and Effect of the banefull Neceffitarian Nightfhade. 'Tis the *Felix Malum*,

————Quo non præsentius ullum
(Pocula fi quando fævæ infecere Novercæ,
Mifcueruntque Herbas, et non innoxia Verba)
Auxilium venit, ac Membris agit atra Venena*.

But tho' Mr. John Wefley is the Vender, and the oftenfible Proprietor, of this efficacious threepeny Medicine; the original Difcovery of the Noftrum is by no Means *his own*. He appears to have pilfer'd the Subftance, both of his *Arcana medendi*, and of his Cavils againft the true Philofophy of *Colors*, from the refuted Lucubrations with which a certain North-Britifh Profeffor hath edify'd and enriched the Literary Public. Let the fimple, however, be on their Guard, left Mr. Wefley's

---

* Georgic. L. 2. 127.

[vi]

Wesley's spiritual Medicines have as pernicious Influence on their Minds; as the quack Remedy, which he * recommends for the Gout, had on the

* In Mr. Wesley's Book of Receipts, entitled *Primitive Physic*, he advises Persons, who have the Gout in their Feet or Hands, to *apply raw lean Beef Steaks* to the Part affected, fresh and fresh every twelve Hours. Somebody recommended this dangerous Repellent, to Dr. *T*, in the Year 1764, or early in 1765. He tryed the Experiment. The Gout was, in consequence, driven up to his Stomach and Head. And he dyed, a few Days after, at *Bath*: where I happen'd to spend a considerable Part of those Years; and where, at the very Time of the Dean's Death, I became acquainted with the Particulars of that Catastrophe.

I am far from meaning to insinuate, because I do not know, that the Person, who persuaded Dr. *T*. to this fatal Recourse, derived the Recipe immediately from Mr. Wesley's medical Compilation. All I aver, is, that the Recipe itself is to be found there. Which demonstrates the unskilfull Temerity, wherewith the Compiler sets himself up as a Physician of the Body. Should his quack Pamphlet come to another Edition, 'tis to be hoped that the *Beef Steak* Remedy will, after so authentic and so melancholy a *probatum est*, be expunged from the List of Specifics for the Gout.— 'Tis, I acknowledge, an effectual Cure. Cut off a Man's Head, and he'll no more be annoy'd by the Tooth-ach.— Alas, for the *Ingenium velox*, and for the *Audacia perdita*, with which a rash Empiric, like Juvenal's *Græculus esuriens*, lays Claim to universal Science!

*Grammaticus, Rhetor, Geometres, Pictor, Aliptes,
Augur, Schænobates, Medicus, Magus! Omnia novit!*

Life

Life of Dr. T——d, the late worthy Dean of N——ch.

By Way of direct Introduction to the following Sheets, allow me to præmife an Extract from the Commentary of a very great Man on thofe celebrated Lines of Juvenal:

Nullum Numen habes fi fit Pudentia; fed te Nos facimus, FORTUNA, *Deam, Cæloque locamus.*

" Dicit autem hoc Poëta, ob *Fortunam:* quæ non
" folum *nullum numen* eft, fed *nufquam* et *nihil* eft.
" Nam, cùm fciamus omnia in Mundo, maxima
" et minima, PROVIDENTIÂ DEI gubernari; quid
" reftat de Fortunâ, nifi vanum et inane No-
" men?———— Unde, recte dicitur, *Tolle* IG-
" NORANTIAM *è Perfonis,* FORTUNAM *de Rebus fuf-*
" *tuleris.* Quia enim Homines Rerum omnium
" Caufas non perfpicimus, ut eft mortalium
" Cæcitas: Fortunam nefcio quam vagam, irri-
" tam, inftabilem, nobis fingimus. Quòd fi
" Caufas Rerum latentes & abditas nobis infpi-
" cere daretur; non modò nullam effe talem For-
" tunam videremus, verùm etiam omnium mini-
" ma, fingulari Dei Providentiâ, regi. Et fic For-
" tuna nihil aliud eft, quàm Dei Providentia, fed
" nobis non perfpecta. Et recte divinus ille *Se-*
" *neca:* FORTUNA, FATUM, NATURA, OMNIA
" EJUSDEM DEI NOMINA, VARIE SUA POTES-
" TATE

" TATE UTENTIS *." i. e. '*The Poet, in this Place, levels his Arrow at* FORTUNE, *or* CHANCE: *which is not only* NO GODDESS, *but a mere* NOTHING, *and has no Existence any where. For since it is certain, that All Things in the World, both little and great, are conducted by the* PROVIDENCE *of* GOD; *what is* Chance, *but an empty, unmeaning Name? Hence it has been rightly observed,* Take away Man's IGNORANCE, *and* CHANCE vanishes in a Moment. *The true Reason, why any of us are for setting up Chance and Fortune, is, our not being always able to* DISCERN *and to* TRACE *the genuine Causes of Events: in consequence of which, we blindly and absurdly feign to ourselves a supposed random, unreal, unsteady Cause, called* LUCK, *or* CONTINGENCY. *Whereas, were we endued with sufficient Penetration to look into the hidden Sources of Things; we should not only see that there is no such Power, as* Contingency, *or Fortune; but, so far from it, that even the* SMALLEST *and most trivial Incidents are guided and governed by* GOD's *own express and special* PROVIDENCE. *If, therefore, the Word,* CHANCE, *have any determinate Signification at all; it can mean neither more nor less than the* UNSEEN MANAGEMENT *of God.*

* LUBINI Comment. in JUVENAL. Sat. 10. P. 454. Edit. Hanoviæ, 1619.

In which Senfe, the admirable Seneca *makes Ufe of the Term:* FORTUNE *(fays that Philofopher)* and FATE, and NATURE, are but fo many different Names of the One true GOD, confider'd as exerting His Power in various Ways and Manners.'—But, with Seneca's good Leave, as the Words *Fortune, Chance, Contingency,* &c. have gradually open'd a Door to the groffeft ATHEISM; and as they require much Subtilty and Prolixity of Explanation, in Order to their being underftood in any other than an ATHEISTICAL Senfe; it is more than expedient, that the Words themfelves fhould be totally and finally cafhier'd and thrown afide.

I have only to add, that if, in the fucceding Effay, any Reader fhould imagine I exprefs my Meaning with *too much Plainnefs*; it may fuffice, to obferve, that there is no End, to the capricious Refinements of affected and exceffive Delicacy.

Quod VERUM, *atque* DECENS, *curo, & rogo, & omnis in hoc fum.*

Language, like animal Bodys, may be phyfic'd, 'till it has no Strength left. We may whet it's Edge, as the Fool fharpen'd his Knife, and as fome are now for reforming the Church, 'till we have whetted the whole Blade away.

BROAD HEMBURY, *January* 22, 1775.

The chief ERRATA, which have been noticed, are these.

Page 80, Line 5 of the Note; *read*, opaque.
   Ibid. Line 6. *read*, a Lucid.
P. 132. Line 7 of the Note; for רבו, read כוב.
P. 153. Line 7. *read*, Delegates.
P. 185. Line 3. *read*, so many.
P. 195. Line 11. after *have*, add a Comma.
P. 199. Line 17. *read*, very possibly.

CHAPTER I.

Necessity *defined: and it's Consistency, with voluntary* Freedom, *proved.*

*A*LIQUIS *in omnibus, nullus in singulis.* The Man, who concerns himself in every Thing, bids fair not to make a Figure in any Thing.

Mr. John Wesley is, precisely, this *Aliquis in omnibus.* For, is there a single Subject, in which he has not endeavored to shine?—He is also, as precisely, a *Nullus in singulis.* For, has he shone in any one Subject which he ever attempted to handle?

Upon what Principle can these two Circumstances be accounted for? Only upon that very Principle, at which he so dolefully shakes his Head: viz. the Principle of *Necessity.* The poor Gentleman is, *necessarily,* an universal Meddler: and, as *necessarily,* an universal Miscarryer. Can he *avoid* being either the One or the Other? No. " Why, " then, do you animadvert upon him?"

1. Becaufe I myfelf am as *neceffary* an Agent, as he:—2. Becaufe I love to " *fhoot Folly as it* " *flyes*:"—3. Becaufe, as, on one hand, *it is* NECESSARY *that there fhould be* HERESYS *among**Men; it is no lefs *neceffary*, on the other, that thofe Herefys fhould be diffected, and expofed. Mr. Wefley imagines, that, upon my own Principles, I can be no more than " a *Clock.*" And, if fo, how can I help *ftriking?* He himfelf has, feveral Times, fmarted, for coming too near the Pendulum.

Mr. Wefley's Incompetence to Argument is never more glaringly confpicuous, than when he paddles in *Metaphyfics*. And yet, I fuppofe, that the Man who has modeftly termed himfelf, and in Print too, " *The greateft Minifter in the* " *World*;" does, with equal Certainty, confider himfelf as the *ableft Metaphyfician* in the World. But his Examinations are far too hafty and fuperficial, to enter into the real Merits of Subjects fo extremely abftrufe, and whofe Concatenations are (though invincibly ftrong, yet) fo exquifitly nice and delicate. One Refult of his thus exercifing himfelf in *Matters which are too high* for him, is,

---

* 1 Cor. xi. 19.

that, in many Cases, he decides peremptorily, without having discern'd so much as the true state of the Question; and then sets himself to *speak evil* of Things which, it is very plain, he *does not understand*. Or, (to borrow the language of Mr. Locke), he " knows a little, præsumes a
" great deal, and so jumps to Conclusions."

I appeal, at present, to his " *Thoughts upon* " Necessity." Thoughts, which, though crude and dark as Chaos, are announc'd, according to Custom, with more than Oracular Positiveness: as though his own *Glandula Pinealis* was the single Focus, wherein all the Rays of Divine and Human Wisdom are concentred.

His *Thoughts* open thus.

1. " Is Man a *Free-agent*, or is he *not?*"— Without all Manner of Doubt, he *is*; in a vast Number and Variety of Cases. Nor did I ever, in Conversation, or in Reading, meet with a Person, or an Author, who deny'd it.

But let us, by defining as we go, ascertain what *Free-agency* is. All needless Refinements apart, *Free-agency*, in plain English, is neither more nor less, than *voluntary Agency*. Whatever the Soul does, with the *full Bent of Preference and Desire*; in That, the Soul acts *freely*. For, *Ubi Consensus, ibi Voluntas: &, ubi Voluntas, ibi Libertas.*

I own

I own myself very fond of *Definitions*. I therefore præmise, *what* the NECESSITY is, whose Cause I have undertaken to plead.

It is exactly and diametrically *opposite*, to that which Cicero delivers concerning FORTUNA, or *Chance, Luck, Hap, Accidentality,* and *Contingency*; invented by the Poets of second Antiquity, and, during many Ages, revered as a Deity, by both Greeks and Romans. " Quid est aliud " *Sors*, quid *Fortuna*, quid *Casus*, quid *Eventus*; " nisi quum sic aliquid cecidit, sic evenit, ut vel " NON cadere atque evenire, vel ALITER cadere " atque evenire, potuerit*?" i. e. *Chance, Fortune, Accident, and Uncertain Event, are then said to take place, when a Thing so comes to pass, as that it either might* NOT *have come to pass at all; or might have come to pass,* OTHERWISE *than it does.*

On the contrary, I would define Necessity to be *That, by which, whatever comes to pass* CANNOT BUT *come to pass* (all Circumstances taken into the Account); *and can come to pass in* NO OTHER WAY *or Manner, than it does.* Which co-incides with Aristotle's Definition of Necessity (though, by the Way, he was a Freewiller himself): Το μη ενδεχομενον ΑΛΛΩΣ εχειν, αναγκαιον φαμεν†:

* *Cic.* De Divinat. L. 2.
† Apud *Frommenium*, Lib. 2. Cap. 9.

We call that Necessary, which cannot be otherwise than it is.

Hence the Greeks termed Necessity, Αναΐκη: because αυασσει, it *reigns*, without Exception, over all the Works of God; and because αυασχει, it *retains* and *comprizes* all Things within the Limits of its own Dominion. The Romans called it Necesse, & Necessitas; quasi *ne Cassitas*, because it cannot *fail*, or be made *void*: & quasi *ne Quassitas*, because it cannot be *moved*, or *shaken*, by all the Power of Men*.

I ac-

---

* The immediate Parent, or *Causa Proxima*, of Necessity, is Fate; called, by the Greeks, ειμαρμενη: because it invincibly *distributes* to every Man his Lot. They termed it also πεπρωμενη. because it *bounds, limits, marks out, adjusts, determines,* and præcisely *ascertains*, to each Individual of the human Race, his assigned Portion both of active and passive Life. Fate was likewise sometimes metonymically styled μοιρα, or the *Lot*, i. e. the *Res ipsissimas*, or very Actions and Felicitys and Sufferings, themselves, which fall to every Man's Share.

The Latins called Fate, *Fatum*: either from *fiat*, i. e. from God's saying, *Let such and such a Thing come to pass*: or, simply, *à fando*; from God's *pronouncing* the Existence, the Continuance, the Circumstances, the Times, and whatever else relates to Men and Things.

If we distinguish accurately, this seems to have been the Order, in which the most judicious of the Antients consider'd the whole Matter. First, God:—then, His Will:—then, Fate; or the solemn Ratification of His Will, by

passing

I acquiesce in the old Distinction of Necessity (a Distinction adopted by LUTHER*, and by most of, not to say by all, the sound Reformed Divines), into a *Necessity of* COMPULSION, and a *Necessity of* INFALLIBLE CERTAINTY.—The Necessity of *Compulsion* is prædicated of *inanimate Bodys*; as we say of the Earth (for Instance) that it circuits the Sun, by compulsory Necessity: and, in some Cases, of *reasonable Beings* themselves; viz. when they are forced to do or suffer any Thing, contrary to their Will and Choice.—The Necessity of infallible *Certainty*, is of a very different Kind: and only renders the Event inevitably future, without any compulsory Force on the Will of the Agent. Thus, it was *infallibly certain*, that Judas would betray Christ: he was, therefore, a *necessary*, though a *voluntary*, Actor in that tremendous Business.

passing and establishing it into an unchangeable Decree:—then, CREATION:—then, NECESSITY; i. e. such an indissoluble Concatenation of secondary Causes and Effects, as has a native Tendency to secure the Certainty of all Events, *sicut Unda impellitur Undâ:*—then, PROVIDENCE; i. e. the omnipræsent, omnivigilant, all-directing Superintendency of Divine Wisdom and Power, carrying the whole præconcerted Scheme into actual Execution, by the subservient Mediation of second Causes, which were created for that End.

* Vide *Luther*. De Servo Arbitrio, Sect. 43.—Edit. *Noremb.* 1526.

2. " Are

2. "Are Man's Actions *free*, or *neceſſary?*"—They may be, at one and the ſame Time, free and neceſſary too. When Mr. Weſley is very hungry, or very tired; he is, *neceſſarily*, and yet *freely*, diſpoſed to Food, or Reſt. He can no more *help* being ſo diſpoſed, than a falling Stone can help tending to the Earth. But here lyes the grand Difference. The Stone is a *ſimple* Being, conſiſting of Matter only: and, conſequently, can have no *Will* either to riſe or fall.—Mr. Weſley is a *compound* Being, made up of Matter and Spirit. Conſequently, his Spirit, Soul, or Will, (for I can conceive no real Difference between the Will, and the Soul itſelf) is concerned in ſitting down to Dinner, or in courting Repoſe, when *Neceſſity* impells to either. And I will venture to affirm, what he himſelf cannot deny, that, *neceſſarily* byaſs'd as he is to thoſe mediums of Recruit; he has recourſe to them as *freely* (i. e. as *voluntarily*, and with as much *Appetite*, *Choice*, *Deſire*, and *Reliſh*), as if Neceſſity was quite out of the Caſe: nay, and with abundantly *greater* Freedom and Choice, than if he was *not* ſo neceſſitated and impell'd.

It would be eaſy, to inſtance this obvious Truth, in a Thouſand Particulars: and in Particulars of infinitely greater Moment, than relate to common Life. Let me juſt, *en paſſant*, illuſtrate the Point, from the most grand and important Topic which the whole Compass of Reasoning affords.

It was *necessary* (i. e. absolutely and intrinsecally *inevitable*), 1. That the MESSIAH should be *invariably* * *holy* in all his Ways, and righteous in all his Works:—2. That He should *dye* for the Sins of Men.

Yet Christ, tho', 1. *necessarily* good (so necessarily, that it was *impossible* for Him to be otherwise); was *freely* and *voluntarily* good: else, He could not have declared, with Truth, *My Meat and Drink* [i. e. my Choice, my Appetite, my Desire] *is, to do the Will of Him that sent me, and to finish His Work* †.—2. Though He ‡ *could not avoid* being put to Death,

as

---

* I never knew more than one *Arminian*, who was so tremendously consistent, as to maintain, explicitly and in Words, that *it was* POSSIBLE *for Christ Himself to have* FALLEN *from Grace by Sin, and to have* PERISH'D *everlastingly*. I must, however, do this Gentleman the Justice to add, that He has, for some Years past, been of a better Judgment.—But the shocking Principle itself is necessarily involved in, and invincibly follows upon, the Arminian Scheme of Contingency; whether the Assertors of that Scheme openly avow the Consequence, or no.

† John iv. 34.

‡ To deny the *Necessity* of Christ's Sufferings, i. e. to consider them as *unprædestinated*, and as Things which

might,

as a Sacrifice for Sin; yet He dy'd *voluntarily*, and therefore *freely*. Else, He would not have affirm'd, that He was even *straighten'd*, *'till it was accomplish'd* *: i. e. He *wish'd*, and *long'd*, for the Consummation of His Obedience unto Death.

Need I add any Thing more, to prove that *Freedom* and *Necessity* are not only compatible, but may even co-alesce into absolute Unisons, with each other?

But, " *How* do they thus co-alesce?"—By the wise Appointment of GOD, who is *great in Counsel, and mighty in Working* †. A *Christian* will be satisfy'd with this Answer. And *Philosophy* itself cannot rise to an higher.

---

might, or might *not*, have happen'd; is to annihilate, at one Stroke, the whole Dignity and Importance of the Christian Religion. Scripture is, therefore, extremely careful to inculcate, again, and again, and again, in the strongest and most explicit Terms which Language can supply, that the *Whole* of Christ's Humiliation, even his Death itself, was infallibly and inevitably DECREED. See, among many other Passages, those which occur in the 5th Chapter of this Essay.

* Luke xii. 50.
† Jer. xxxii. 19.

CHAP.

CHAPTER II.

The NECESSITY *of Human Volitions proved, from the Nature of the Connection subsisting between Soul and Body.*

MR. Wesley asks, 3. " Is Man *self*-deter-" min'd, in Acting; or is he determin'd " by *some other* Being?"—I scruple not, to declare, as *my* stedfast Judgement, that no Man ever *was*, or ever *will*, or ever *can* be, strictly and philosophically speaking, *self-determined* to any one Action, be that Action what it may.

Let us examine this Point. It is neither unimportant, nor unentertaining.

There is * no *Medium* between MATTER and SPIRIT. These Two divide the whole Universe between them. Even in Man's present *complex* State, tho' Body and Soul constitute one Compositum; yet are the two component Principles not only distinct, but essentially * different, from

* * I am obliged, here, to take these two Particulars for granted: As the Adhibition of the abundant Proofs, by which they are supported and evinced, would lead me too far from the Object immediately in View.

. each

each other. Their *Connection*, tho' aſtoniſhingly intimate, occaſions no *Mixture* nor *Confuſion* of This with That.

Notwithſtanding which, the Nature (or, if you pleaſe, the Law) of their Junction is ſuch, that they reciprocally *act upon* each other. A Man breaks a Limb: or is wounded in a Duel. The Body, and the Body alone, receives the Injury: but the Injury is no ſooner received, than it operates upon the Soul. For it is the *Soul* only, which *feels* Pleaſure or Pain, through the Medium of the bodily Organs. Matter can no more *feel*, or *perceive*; than it can *read*, or *pray*. To ſuppoſe otherwiſe, were to ſuppoſe that a Violin can hear, and a Teleſcope ſee.

If, therefore, the *Soul* is the feeling Principle, or ſole Seat of Perception; it follows, as clear as Day, that the Soul is no leſs *dependent* on the Body, for a very conſiderable Portion of it's [i. e. of the Soul's own] phyſical Happineſs or Miſery; than the Body is dependent on the Soul, for it's [i. e. for the Body's] inſtrumental Subſerviency to the Will.—Conſequently, the Soul is (not *ſelf-determined*, but) *neceſſarily* determined, to take as much Care of the Body as it [the Soul] in it's preſent Views deems requiſit: becauſe the Soul is *conſcious* of it's Dependence on that Machine, as the Inlet and Channel of pleaſ-

ing

ing or of difagreeable Senfations. So that, in this very extenfive Inftance, Man's *Volitions* are fwayed, this way or that, to the right hand or to the left; by Confiderations, drawn from the Circumftance of that *neceffary* Dependence on the Body, which the Soul cannot poffibly raife itfelf fuperior to, while the mutual Connection fubfifts.

An *Idea* is that *Image, Form, or Conception of any Thing, which the Soul is impreffed with from without* *. How come we by thefe Ideas? I believe them to be, all, originally, let in, through the bodily *Senfes* only. I cannot confider *Reflection* as, properly, the Source of any new Ideas: but rather as a fort of mental Chemiftry, by which the Underftanding contemplatively analyfes and fublimates, into abftract and refined Knowledge, fome of thofe Ideas which refult either from Experience, or from Information; and which were primarily admitted through

* Are not the Powers of *Fancy* an Exception to that Doctrine which maintains, that all Ideas originally accede, *ab extra*, to the Mind? — Not in the leaft. Tho' I may form (for Inftance) an uncertain, or at beft an incomplete, Idea of a Perfon I never faw; yet that Idea is either drawn from Defcription, or, if purely imaginary, is a Combination of Conceptions, every one of which came at firft into the Mind through the Senfes, and which it affociates on Principles of real or fuppofed Similitude.

the

the Avenues of Senfe. Without the Senfe of Hearing, we could have had no juft Idea of Sound; nor of Odors, without the Senfe of Smelling: any more than the Foot can tafte, or the Hand can hear.

The Senfes themfelves, which are thus the only Doors, by which Ideas, i. e. the Rudiments of all * Knowledge, find their Way to the Soul; are, literally and in the fulleft Import of the Word, *corporeal*. Hence, the Soul cannot *see*, if the Eyes are deftroy'd: nor *feel*, if the nervous Functions are fufpended: nor *hear*, if the Organs of that Senfe are totally impair'd. What learn we from this? That the Soul, or Mind, is primarily and immediately indebted to the Body, for all the *Ideas* (and, confequently, for all the *Knowledge*) with which it is furnifhed. By thefe

---

* The Reader will obferve, that I am, here, fpeaking of no other than of *natural* and of *artificial* Knowledge. *Spiritual* Knowledge, divinely imprefs'd on the Soul in it's. Regeneration by the HOLY GHOST, comes not, hitherto, within the Compafs of the prefent Difquifition. Tho', to me, it feems extremely probable, that this moft adorable Agent often condefcends to make the Senfes themfelves (and efpecially the Senfe of Feeling; to which fingle Senfe, by the Way, all the other Four may, *sub diverso Modo*, be reduced) the Inlets of His Bleffed Influence. *There is a Spirit in Man: and the Infpiration of the Almighty giveth them Underftanding.* Job xxxii. 8.

Ideas,

Ideas, when compared, combined, or separated; the Soul, on every Occasion, *necessarily* regulates it's Conduct: and is afterwards as dependent on the Body for carrying it's Conceptions into outward Act, as it was for it's simple Reception of them at first.

Thus, the Soul is, in a very extensive Degree, *passive* as Matter itself.

Whether the Fibres of the Brain do no more than *simply* vibrate; or whether they be *also* the Canals of a vital Fluid *agitated* and set in Circulation, by the Percussions which it receives from the Senses; the Argument comes to just the same Point. The Senses are *necessarily* impress'd by every Object from without; and as *necessarily* commove the Fibres of the Brain: from which nervous Commotion, *Ideas* are necessarily communicated to, or excited in, the Soul; and, by the Judgement which the Soul necessarily frames of those Ideas, the Will is necessarily inclined to approve or disapprove, to act or not to act. If so, where is the boasted Power of Self-determination?

Having taken a momentary Survey of the Soul's *Dependence* on the Body; and of the vast Command which the Body has over the Soul (so great, that a *Disease* may quickly degrade a Philosopher into an Ideot; and even an Alteration

of

of * *Weather* diffuse a temporary Stupor through all the Powers of the Mind); let us next enquire,

---

* Lord Chesterfield's Remark is not ill founded. "I am "convinced, that a light Supper, a good Night's Sleep, "and a fine Morning; have, sometimes, made an Hero, "of the same Man, who, by an Indigestion, a restless "Night, and a rainy Morning, would have been a Coward." *Letter* 117.—Again: "Those who see and observe Kings, "Heros, and Statesmen, discover that they have Head-"achs, Indigestions, Humors, and Passions, just like other "People: every one of which, in their Turns, determine "their Wills, in Defiance of their Reason." *Letter* 173.— Human Excellence, truly, has much to be proud of! And Man is a Sovereign, *self-determining* Animal! An Animal, whom too rarify'd or too viscous a Texture, too rapid or too languid a Circulation, of *Blood*; an imperfect Secretion of *Spirits*, from the Blood, through the cortical Strainers of the Brain; or an irregular Distribution of the spiritous Fluid, from the secreting Fibres, to the nervous Canals which diffuse themselves through the Body:—these, and a thousand other involuntary Causes, can, at any Time, in less than a Moment, if GOD please, suspend every one of our Sensations; stagnate us into Stupidity; agitate us into a Fever; or deprive us of Life itself!

Yet, let it be observ'd, that *Thought* and *Reason* are, at all Times and amidst all Circumstances whatever, *essentially inseparable* from the SOUL: whether it dwell in a well-organized and duly-temper'd Body, or in a Body whose Construction is ever so unfavorable, and whose mechanic Balance is ever so broken and impaired. But, in the latter Case (especially in Swoons, Epilepsys, &c.) the Soul cannot *unfold*

quire, on what the *Body itself* depends, for the Sources of those innumerable Ideas, which it is the

fold and *exercise* it's Facultys, as when the material Machine is in right Order. Thus, we cannot say, with metaphysical Propriety, that a Person in a *fainting-fit*, or that even the most absolute *Ideot* on Earth, is an *irrational* Being: but only, that he has not the *Service* of his Reason. Nor can we say, of a Madman, that he has *lost* his Understanding: but only, that the proper *Use*, or *Direction*, of it, is perverted.

'Tis true, indeed, that, as *Ideotcy* seems to be rather a *quid deficiens*, than a το *positivum*; and may therefore be immediately occasion'd by the bad Mechanism (i. e. by a vitiated Arrangement and Motion) of the corporeal Particles, whether fluid or solid:—So, on the other Hand, *Madness* seems to have more in it of the το *positivum*; and, consequently, to be the Effect of an higher and more absolute Cause. What can that Cause be? I am strongly and clearly of opinion, with Mr. Baxter (not Baxter the old Puritan, but Baxter the great modern Philosopher), that all *Madness* whatever procedes from the powerfull and continued Agency of some separate Spirit, or Spirits, obtruding phantastic Visions on the Soul of the insane Person. If the Majority of Dreams are but the Madness of Sleep, what is Madness, properly so called, but a waking Dream? For, as that most accomplished Metaphysician very justly reasons, " The " Soul, in itself, is an uncompounded, simple Substance, " and hath no Parts, and therefore properly *no Constitution*: " neither is it liable to *any Change*, or *Alteration*, in it's own " Nature. The *inert Matter* of the Body could never affect " it thus [i. e. could never so affect the Soul, as to occa- " sion

the Vehicle of tranſmitting to the Intellect: and, without which Tranſmiſſion, the Intellect, im-
plunged

"ſion Madneſs]. *That* could only *limit* the Facultys of the Soul, farther and farther, or *deaden* it's Activity: but not *animate* it after ſuch a *terrible* Manner. Hence there is no other Way for it's being affected *in this* Manner, but the *Cauſe* I have already aſſigned. — — —
There is, indeed, a great Difference, and Variety, in the Phænomena of *Reaſon diſturbed*. But, univerſally, the *Diſeaſe* could not be lodged in the Soul itſelf: nor could the *Matter* of the Body affect it any other Way, than by *deadening* [i. e. by impeding] it's Activity; which, I think, is never the Caſe in theſe Appearances. In ſhort, the Diſorder of *Matter* might make a Man a *ſtupid Idiot*; ſubject him to *Sleep, Apoplexy*, or any Thing approaching to it's own Nature: but could never be the Cauſe of *Rage*, *Diſtraction, Phrenſy*, unleſs it were employed as an Inſtrument by *ſome other Cauſe:* that is, *It cannot of itſelf be the Cauſe* of theſe Diſorders of Reaſon. If the *Inertia* of Matter infers any Thing, it infers thus much."
BAXTER's *Enquiry into the Nature of the human Soul*, Vol. II. p. 141, 142.—I no more doubt, that Mad Perſons, at this very Day, are *Dæmoniacs*, or influenced and agitated by incorporeal and inviſible Beings; than I can doubt, that ſome People were ſo *poſſeſſed*, at the Time of our Lord's Abode on Earth. Such an Aſſertion will, probably, ſound romantically ſtrange, to a præjudiced, and to a ſuperficial, Ear. But (let the *Fact* itſelf really ſtand how it may), I think I can venture to pronounce, that the *Philoſophy* of the *Opinion*, as ſtated and argued by Mr. Baxter, is irrefragable. —Examine firſt, and then judge.

C   Unembody'd

plunged in a Mass of Clay, could have had no more Idea of outward Things, than an Oyster has

Unembody'd Spirits, both friendly and hostile (ευδαιμονες, & κακοδαιμονες), holy and unholy, have more to do with us, in a Way both of Good and Evil, than the Generality of us seem to imagine. But they themselves are, All, no more than Parts of that great Chain, which depends on the First Cause, or Uncreated Link: and can only act as Ministers of HIS Will.

Luther relates several uncommon Things, concerning his own Converse with some of the spiritual World: which, however fanciful they may, *primâ facie*, appear; are by no means philosophically inadmissible. For so saying, I am sure to incurr a Smile of Contempt, from Pertlings and Materialists: the former of whom *sneer*, when they cannot *reason*; and wisely consider a *Grin*, and a *Syllogism*, as two Names for the same Thing. When it can be solidly proved, that the Gums are the Seat of Intellect; I will then allow, that a Laugher shews his Understanding and his Wit, every Time he shews his Teeth. Was *Ridicule* the legitimate *Test of Truth*, there could be no such Thing as Truth in the World; and, consequently, there would be nothing for Ridicule to be the Test of: as *every* Truth *may be*, and in it's Turn *actually has been*, ridiculed, by some insipid Witling or other. So that, to borrow a lively Remark from Mr. Hervey, " The Whim, of making Ridicule the Test of " Truth, seems as suitable to the Fitness of Things, as to " place Harlequin in the Seat of Lord Chief Justice." Moreover, *Ridicule* itself, view'd as *ridiculously* usurping the Office of a philosophical Touch-stone; has been *ridiculed*, with

has of a Tinder-box. An unactive Confcioufnefs of mere torpid Exiftence would have been the whole Amount of it's Riches, during it's Inclofure in a Prifon without Door, Window, or Crevice.

The human Body is *neceffarily* encompafs'd by a Multitude of *other* Bodys. Which other furrounding Bodys (animal, vegetable, &c.), fo far as we come within their perceivable Sphære, *neceffarily* imprefs our Nerves with Senfations correfpondent to the Objects themfelves. Thefe Senfations are *neceffarily* (and, for the moft Part, *inftantaneoufly*) propagated to the Soul: which

with much Poignancy, and Strength of Senfe, by the ingenious Pen of the late Dr. Brown, in his *Effay on Satire:*

" Come, let us join awhile this titt'ring Crew,
And own, the Ideot Guide for once is true:
Deride our weak Forefathers' mufty Rule,
Who therefore fmiled, becaufe they faw a Fool.
Sublimer Logic now adorns our Ifle:
We therefore fee a Fool, becaufe we fmile!
  Truth in her gloomy Cave why fondly feek?
Lo, gay fhe fits in *Laughter*'s dimple Cheek:
Contemns each furly Academic Foe,
And courts the fpruce Free-thinker and the Beau.
  No more fhall REASON boaft her Pow'r divine:
Her Bafe eternal fhook by *Folly*'s Mine.
TRUTH's facred Fort th' exploded *Laugh* fhall win;
And Coxcombs vanquifh *Berkley* by a GRIN!"

can no more *help* receiving them and being affected by them, than a Tree can refist a Stroke of Lightening.

Now, (1.) if all the *Ideas* in the Soul derive their Exiftence from *Senfation*; and, (2.) if the Soul depend, abfolutely, on the *Body*, for all thofe Senfations; and, (3.) if the Body be both primarily and continually dependent, on other extrinfec Beings, for the very Senfations which it [the Body] communicates to the Soul; — the Confequence feems, to me, undeniable: that neither the immanent nor the tranfient Acts of Man (i. e. neither his mental, nor his outward Operations) are *felf*-determin'd; but, on the contrary, determined by the Views with which an Infinity of furrounding Objects *neceffarily*, and almoft inceffantly, imprefs his Intellect.

And on *what* do thofe furrounding *Objects themfelves*, which are moftly material (i. e. on what does Matter, in all it's Forms, Pofitions, and Relations), depend? Certainly, not on Itfelf. It could neither be it's own Creator, nor can it be it's own Conferver. In my Idea, every Particle of Matter would immediately revert into Non-exiftence, if not retained in Being, from Moment to Moment, by the Will of HIM who *upholds all Things by the Word of his Power**, and *through Whom all Things confift*†.

* Heb. i. 3.   † Col. i. 17.

Much

Much lefs, does Matter depend on the Human Mind. Man can neither create, nor * exterminate, a fingle Atom. There are Cafes, wherein he can *alter* the Modes of Matter: fo as to form (for Inftance) certain vegetable Fibres into Linen, Linen into Paper, and Paper into Books. He can alfo throw that Linen, or Paper, or Books, into a Fire; and thereby diffolve the prefent *connection* of their Particles, and annihilate their *modal Relations*. But, notwithftanding he has all this in his *Power*, (tho', by the Way, he'll never *do* either one or the other, except his *Will* be *neceffarily* determined by fome effectual Motive); ftill, the feeming Deftruction amounts to no more than a Variation. Not an individual Particle of the burnt Matter is extermin'd: nor even it's effential Relation, to the Univerfe, fu-

---

* To all her other antiphilofophical Abfurditys, *Arminianifm* adds the fuppofed *Defectibility* of faving Grace: by giving as her Opinion, that the Holy Principle in a renewed Soul is not only a *corruptible* and *perifhable* Seed, but that it, frequently, and actually, *does* fuffer a *total Extinction* and a *final Annihilation*. Or, as Mr. Wefley and his Fraternity vulgarly exprefs it, " He who is, to-day, a Child of God, " may be, to-morrow, a Child of the Devil." As if the Principle of Grace were lefs privileged than a Particle of Matter! And as if Man, who cannot annihilate a fingle Atom, were able to annihilate the moft illuftrious Effect of the Holy Spirit's Operation! *Credat Judæus*, &c.

C 3 perfeded.

perseded. There would be, præcisely, the same Quantity of solid Substance, which there now is, without the Loss of a corpuscular Unit; were all the Men, and Things, upon the Face of the Earth, and the very Globe itself, reduced to Ashes. Consequently, Matter is absolutely and solely dependent on God himself.

Thus have we, briefly, traced the winding Current to it's Source. The SOUL, or Intellect, depends on it's *Ideas*, for the Determinations of its *Volitions:* else, it would will, as a blind Man walks, at a Venture and in the Dark.—Those Ideas are the Daughters of *Sensation*; and can deduce their Pedigree from no other Quarter. The embody'd Soul could have had no Idea of so much as a Tree, or a Blade of Grass, if our Distance from those Bodys had been such, as to have præcluded their respective Forms from occurring to the Eye.—The *Senses*, therefore, are the Channels of all our natural Perceptions. Which Senses are entirely *corporeal:* as is the *Brain* also, that grand Centre, to which all their Impressions are forwarded, and from whence they immediately act upon the Immaterial Principle.—These corporeal Senses receive their Impressions from the Presence, or Impulse, of *exterior Beings* (for all our Sensations are but Modes of Motion).—And every one of those exterior Beings is dependent,

for

for Existence, and for Operation, on GOD Most High.

Such is the Progression of one Argument (and 'tis but one among many), for the great Doctrine of Philosophical Necessity: A Chain, concerning which (and, especially, concerning the Determination to Action, by Motives arising from Ideas) Mr. *Wesley* modestly affirms, that " It has not one good Link belonging to it." Seriously, I pity the Size of his Understanding. And I pity it, because I verily believe it to be a `Fault which he *cannot help*: any more than a Dwarf can help not being Six Feet high. Lame indeed are all his Commentations:

" *But better he'd give us, if better he had.*"

I shall close this Chapter, with submitting a few plain and reasonable Quærys to the Reader.

1. How is that Supposition, which ascribes a *Self-determining Will* to a created Spirit; less ABSURD, than that Supposition, which ascribes *Self-Existence* to Matter?

2. In what Respect, or Respects, is the Arminian Supposition of a *fortuitous Train of Events*; less ATHEISTICAL, than the Epicuræan Supposition of a *fortuitous Concourse of Atoms*?

3. If

3. If Man be a *Self-determining* Agent; will it not neceſſarily follow, that there are as many *Firſt Cauſes* (i.e. in other Words, as many GODS), as there are MEN in the World?

4. Is not *Independence* eſſentially præerequiſit to *Self-determination*?

5. But is it true in FACT, and would it be found PHILOSOPHY to admit, that *Man* is an *independent Being*?

6. Moreover, is the Suppoſition, of *Human Independence* and *Self-determination*, ſound THEOLOGY? At leaſt, does it comport with the *Scriptural* Account of Man? For a Specimen of which Account, only caſt your Eye on the Paſſage or two that follow.—*The Way of Man is not in himſelf: it is not in Man that walketh to direct his own Steps* *.—*Without Me* [i. e. without Chriſt], *ye can do nothing* †.—*In Him* [i. e. in God] *we live, and are moved* (κινυμεθα), *and have our Exiſtence* ‡.—*It is He who worketh All in All* §.—*It is God, who worketh in you both to will and to do* ‖.—*Of Him, and to Him, and through Him, are all Things* ¶.

7. May we not, on the whole, ſoberly affirm; that the Scheme of Neceſſity is *Philoſophy in her*

---

* Jer. x. 23. † John xv. 5.
‡ Acts xvii. 28. § 1 Cor. xii. 6.
‖ Phil. ii. 13. ¶ Rom. xi. 36.

right Mind? And, that the Scheme of Contingency is *Philofophy run mad?*

CHAPTER III.

Several OBJECTIONS, *to the Scheme of* NECESSITY, *anfwered.*

IT feems moft agreeable to the radical Simplicity, which God has obferved in His Works; to fuppofe, that, *in themfelves,* All human Souls are *equal.* I can eafily believe, that the Soul of an Oyfter-woman has, naturally, the (unexpanded) Powers of *Grotius,* or of Sir *Ifaac Newton:* and that what conduces to raife the Philofopher, the Poet, the Politician, or the Linguift, fo much above the ignorant and ftupid of Mankind; is, not only the Circumftance of intellectual Cultivation, but (ftill more than That) his having the Happinefs to occupy a better Houfe, i. e. a *Body* more commodioufly *organized,* than They.

The Soul of a *Monthly Reviewer,* if imprifon'd within the fame mud Walls which are tenanted by the Soul of Mr. *John Wefley;* would, fimilarly circumftanced, reafon and act (I verily think) exactly

exactly like the Bishop of Moor-fields. And I know some very sensible People, who even go so far, as to suppose, that, was an Human Spirit shut up in the Skull of a *Cat*; Puss would, notwithstanding, move prone on all four, purr when stroaked, spit when pinched, and Birds and Mice be her darling Objects of Persuit.

Now, tho' I can, by no means, for my own Part, carry Matters to so extreme a Length as this; yet, I repeat my Opinion, that Much, very Much, depends on corporeal Organization. Whence the usual Remark, that a Man is (I would rather say, appears to be) sensible and ingenious, according to his Dimension and solid Content of Brain. That is, as I apprehend, the Soul is more capable of *exerting* it's Powers, when lodg'd in a capacious and well-constructed Vehicle. I dare believe, that the Brain of Dr. *Thomas Nowell* is, to That of Mr. *John Wesley*, as 2 to 1, at the very least. And yet, all this is the Result of absolute *Necessity*. For, what is Brain, but Matter peculiarly modify'd? And Who is the Modifyer? Not Man, but God.

I just now hinted the Conjecture of some, that an human Spirit, incarcerated in the Brain of a Cat; would, probably, both think and behave, as that Animal now does. But how would

would the * Soul of a Cat acquit itſelf, if in-
cloſed in the Brain of a Man? We cannot re-
ſolve this Quæſtion, with *Certainty*, any more
than the other. We may, however, even on
this Occaſion, addreſs every one of our human
Brethren in thoſe Words of that great philoſo-
phic Neceſſitarian, St. Paul; and aſk, *Who maketh thee to differ* from the loweſt of the Brute
Creation? Thy MAKER's Free-will, not thine.—
And what Præ-eminence *haſt thou, which thou
didſt not receive* from Him? Not the leaſt, nor

---

* Let not the Reader ſtart, at that Expreſſion, ' The *Soul*
' of a Cat.' For tho' the Word, ſo apply'd, may ſeem
ſtrange to thoſe who have not weighed both Sides of the
Quæſtion (it would have ſeemed very ſtrange to *me*, about
15 Years ago); yet, on giving the Cauſe an impartial
Hearing, the Scale of Evidence will, in my Judgement,
ſtrongly decide for an *Immaterial Principle* in Brutes.

I mean not, here, to diſcuſs the Argument. But let me
hint, that one principal Hinge, on which the Enquiry turns,
is: *Do thoſe inferior Beings* REASON, *or do they* NOT? If
they *do* (be it in ever ſo ſmall a Degree), they muſt conſiſt
of ſomething more than Body: i. e. they muſt be com-
pounded of *Matter* AND *Spirit*.—If they do *not* reaſon at all
(and we may as well doubt whether they can *feel* at all);
we may ſet them down for mere material Machines.—He,
however, who ſeriouſly thinks, that even Birds, or Inſects,
are *Watches*; may, with equal Eaſe, while his Hand is in,
advance a few Steps higher, and ſuppoſe, that Men are
Clocks, i. e. larger Watches of the three.

the Shadow of any.——*Now, if thou didſt* [not *acquire,* but] *receive it,* as a diſtinguiſhing Gift of His free and ſovereign Pleaſure ; *why carryeſt thou thyſelf proudly* (καυχασαι), *as tho' thou hadſt not received it* * ?

" He, who through vaſt Immenſity can pierce ;
" See Worlds on Worlds compoſe one Univerſe ;
" Can tell how Syſtem beyond Syſtem runs ;
" What other Planets circle other Suns ;
" What vary'd Being peoples ev'ry Star :
" May tell, Why Heav'n has made us as we are."

What the Poet could not tell, the Bible does.—
" Why are we made as we are?" *Even ſo, Father: for ſo it ſeemed good in Thy Sight.* Which is Anſwer enough to ſatisfy *me.*

 I take the Truth of the Matter to be this. All the intellectual Diſtinctions, which obtain, throughout the whole Scale of animated Exiſtence, from the brighteſt Angel down to Man, and which give Advantage to one Man above another; which intellectual Diſtinctions deſcend, likewiſe, in juſt Gradations, from Man, to the minuteſt Animalcule ;—are diſtributed, to each Individual, *in Number, in Meaſure, and in Weight* †, by the

* 1 Cor. iv. 7.   † Wiſd. xi. 20.

ſovereign

sovereign Will and the unerring Hand of GOD *the only Wise*. The Uses, to which those intellectual Powers shall subserve; the Term of their Duration; and, in short, every Circumstance relative both to *them* and their *Possessors*; I consider as falling under the Regulation of God's determining and permissive DECREE *before* Time, and of His ever-present and ever-active PROVIDENCE *in* Time.

According to this Scheme of Things (a Scheme, which, when fairly weighed, will be found the most chearfull to Men, and the most worthy of God, which was ever proposed to the Human Mind); that melancholy, that absurd, that atheistical Fiction, whose Name is *Chance*, has nothing to do with God or with His Works. On the contrary, the golden Chain of NECESSITY, PROVIDENCE, or FATE ('tis no Matter which you term it), is let down, from the Throne of the Supreme, through all the Ranks of animated and of unanimated Creation: guiding and governing every Individual Spirit, and every Individual Atom, by such Means, and in such a Manner, as best comport with the Dignity, the Efficacy, the Wisdom, and the Love, of HIM who *holds* the Chain, and who has *implicated* every Link.

Thus, *He doth according to His Will, in the Armys of Heaven, and among the Inhabitants of the*

the Earth; and none can stay His Hand, or say unto Him, What dost thou *? Hence it is, that the very † *Hairs* of our Heads are, *all, number'd* in His Book; and not one of them can fall from it's Pore, without the Leave of Heaven. He is the Guardian of † *Sparrows*; and will not let what we account the meanest Insect expire, 'till the Point of Time, divinely destined, is come. He not only tells the Number of the ‡ *Stars*, and calls them each by Name; but notices and directs the very Particles of § *Dust*, which float in the Atmosphere. The ‖ *Sun* shines not, but at His Command: nor can a ¶ *Wind* blow, but by Authority from Him.——May we not say, of Necessity, what the Psalmist says, of the central Luminary, round which our Globe is wheel'd; that *there is nothing hid from the Heat thereof?*

And yet, there are Those, who think, that *Necessity* makes no Part of the *Christian* System!

Mr. *Wesley* is, or pretends to be, of this Number. Let us give a concise Hearing to the Difficultys, which, in his Estimation, clog the Scheme of evangelical and philosophical Fate:

* Dan. iv. 35.   † Matth. x. 29, 30.
‡ Psalm cxlvii. 4.   § Isaiah xl. 12.
‖ Job ix. 7.   ¶ Psalm cxxxv. 7.

tho'

tho' they are such as have been refuted again and again.

1. " There can be no moral Good, or Evil; " no Virtue, and no Vice."

So thought * *Aristotle*; and his Disciples, the *Peripatetics*. Hence, they defined Moral Virtue to be an *elective* Habit, flowing originally from *Free-will*, and render'd easy by repeated Acts.

It is no Wonder, that proud Heathens should thus *err*; seeing they *knew not the Scriptures, nor the Power of God*. But Mr. Wesley should remember, that *he* has read, and professes to believe, a Book which tells him, that *a Man can receive nothing, except it be given him from Heaven*†; that we cannot even *think a good Thought*‡, unless God breathe it into our Hearts; and that it is *the Father of our Lord Jesus Christ*, who must *work in us that which is well-pleasing in His Sight* §.

---

* And yet Aristotle, tho' a *vehement*, was not (any more than his Disciple of the Foundery) a *consistent*, Freewillman. Hence, Aristotle, being once asked, " Who can " keep a Secret?" made this odd Answer: *He that can hold red-hot Coals in his Mouth.*—Surely, *Freewill* must be very feeble, and *Necessity* irresistibly potent, upon this Principle! Not to ask: If Freewill cannot, on a proper Occasion, shut the Mouth of the Man that has it; how can it bring him Virtue, and save his Soul?

† John iii. 27. ‡ 2 Cor. iii. 5. § Hebr. xiii. 21.

Nor

Nor should his Lordship of Moor-fields forget, that he has solemnly subscribed (to omit all present Mention of *Articles* and *Homilys*) a certain *Liturgy:* in which Liturgy, among a Thousand other Passages equally excellent, G O D Himself is addressed, as the sole Being, *From whom* ALL *holy* DESIRES, *all good* COUNSELS [or sincerely devout Intentions], *and all* JUST WORKS, *do procede.* The Supreme is, likewise, in that same " Calvinistical and Antinomian Prayer-book," declared to be the *Almighty and ever-living God, who* MAKETH *us both to* WILL *and to* DO *those Things that be* GOOD *and acceptable to his divine Majesty.* And, in absolute Harmony with this *necessitating* Principle, the said Book beseeches the Blessed Father and Governor of Men, that, *By* HIS *holy* INSPIRATION, *we may* THINK *those Things that are good*; and that we may, *by* HIS *mercifull* GUIDANCE, *faithfully* PERFORM *the same.* If this is being, what Mr. Wesley terms, " a fine " Piece of *Clock-work;*" I heartily wish and pray, that *I* may, every Hour of my Life, be *so* wound up.

But still, says the Objector, " Moral Good, or " Evil," cannot * consist with Necessity. I, on

the

---

* " The hackney'd Objection to the Doctrine of Ne-
" cessity, from it's being [pretendedly] *inconsistent with the*
" *Idea*

the contrary, say, that it both *can*, and *does*. Mr. Wesley does not consider the tremendous consequences, which unavoidably flow from his Position. For, if *necessary* Virtue be neither *moral*, nor *praise-worthy*; 'twill follow, That God Himself (who, without all Doubt, is *necessarily* and unchangeably Good) is an *immoral* Being, and *not Praise-worthy* for his Goodness! On the same horrible Arminian Principle, 'twould also follow, that Christ's most perfect Obedience (which was *necessary:* for He *could not but* obey perfectly) had *no Morality* in it, was totally *void of Merit*, and entitled Him to neither *Praise*, nor *Reward!* The Axiom, therefore, which dares to affirm, that " Necessity and Moral Agency are irrecon-
" cilable Things;" lays, at once, an Axe to the Root both of natural and revealed Religion, and

" *Idea of Virtue and Vice, as implying Praise and Blame*;
" may be fully retorted upon it's Opponents. For, as to
" their boasted *Self-determining Power* (were the Thing *pos-*
" *sible* in itself, and did not imply an *Absurdity*), by which
" they pretend to have a Power of acting *independently* of
" every Thing that comes under the Description of *Motive*;
" I scruple not to say, that it is as foreign to every Idea of
" Virtue or Vice, Praise or Blame, as the grossest Kind
" of Mechanism that the most blundering Writer in De-
" fence of Liberty ever ascribed to the Advocates for moral
" Necessity."
Dr. *Priestley*'s Exam. of Beattie, &c. p. 178.

D ought

ought to be hiffed back again by all Mankind to the Hell from whence it came.

The Crucifyers of the Son of God perpetrated the *moſt immoral Act*, that ever was, or ever will be, committed. And yet, I am expreſsly aſſured, by the written Teſtimony of the Holy Ghoſt, enter'd on a Record which will continue to the End of Time, that *Herod, and Pontius Pilate, and the People of the Jews, were gather'd together againſt Jeſus, for to do whatſoever* GOD's Hand *and* GOD's Counſel *had* FORE-DETERMINED *to be done* *. So that, upon *Chriſtian* Principles at leaſt, NECESSITY and MORAL EVIL (by the ſame Rule, alſo, NECESSITY and MORAL GOOD) may walk † hand in hand together. If Mr. Weſley prefers *Ariſtotle* and the other Gentlemen of the *Lycæum*, to the Inſpired Writers; and chuſes the *peripatetic* Scheme of Free-will, rather than the *Bible* Scheme of Neceſſity; he muſt, for me, go on to hug an Idol that cannot ſave.

The whole Cavil amounts to præciſely this. *If God is the alone Author and Worker of all Good; Virtue ceaſes to be Virtue:* And, *If God is the free Permittor of Evil, Vice ceaſes to be Vice.* Can any Thing be, at once, more impious, and more

---

* Acts ii. 23. and iv. 28.

† I have largely canvaſs'd this Point, in a former Tract, entitled, *More Work for Mr. John Weſley.*

irrational,

irrational, than the Letter and the Spirit of these two Propositions?

In one Word: those Modes of Action, called *Virtue* and *Vice*, do not cease to be *moral*, i. e. to affect our *Manners*, as Creatures of God, and as Members of Society; be those Modes occasion'd by what they may. Acts of Devotion, Candor, Justice, and Beneficence, together with their Opposites; are, to all Intents and Purposes, as *morally* good or evil, if they flow from one Source, as from another: tho' no Works can be *evangelically* good and pleasing to God, which do not spring from His own Grace in the Heart. But this latter Circumstance is entirely of *spiritual* Consideration. It has nothing to do, off or on, with the mere * *Morality* of Actions. Good is *morally*, i. e. religiously excellent, or socially beneficial; and Evil is *morally*, i. e. religiously bad or socially injurious; whether Men be self-determining Agents, or not. Light *is* Light, and Darkness *is* Darkness; flow they from the right hand, or from the left.

* *Morality* is, I think, usually, and very justly, defined to be, *That Relation, or Proportion, which Actions bear, to a given Rule.* Consequently, neither Necessity, nor Non-Necessity, has any Thing to do with the Morality of Action.

2. We are told, that, on the Hypothesis of NECESSITY, Man is " neither *rewardable*, nor " *punishable*; neither *praise*-, nor *blame*-worthy."

No Objection can be more unphilosophical than this, because it quite loses sight of the very Point in Debate; viz. of *Necessity* itself: by which, certain Causes *inevitably* produce certain Effects, and certain Antecedents are *inevitably* concatenated with certain Consequences. 'Tis sufficient, therefore, to answer: that the Will of God has established a natural *Connection* between Virtue and * Happiness, Vice and Misery. This divinely establish'd Connection is so indissoluble, that, even in the present State of Things, Happiness never fails to enter at the same Door with Virtue; nor does Misery ever fail to tread upon the Heels of Vice.

Some Sensualists, however, profess otherwise: and affirm, that their own Deviations from the moral Path are neither attended, nor follow'd, by any pungent Briar, or grieving Thorn. Their Draughts are all balmy and nectareous, without a Drop of Wormwood or of Gall, to allay the Sweetness, or to embitter the Remembrance.

Those Gentlemen must, however, excuse me from taking their Word for this. I don't believe

---

* I here speak of *intellectual* Happiness or Misery.

one

one Syllable of it to be true. Both Scripture, and the Nature of the Case, and the Observations I have made; unite to render me quite positive, that *The Way of Transgressors is hard* * : that, even *in the* MIDST *of Laughter*, they have a Tinge of *Sorrow* in their *Hearts*; as well as that *the* END *of* their *Mirth is Heaviness* †. They may, for a Time, like the Lacedæmonian Boy, *conceal* the Wolf that is eating out their very Intrails; and set the Gloss of an outward Sardonian Smile, on the inward Pangs they endure: but the Great Law of NECESSITY, from which neither the Virtuous nor the Licentious are exempt, assures me, that this pretended Ease is mere Dissimulation and Grimace.

One of the most sensible Men I ever knew, but whose Life, as well as his Creed, had been rather excentric; returned me the following Answer, not many Months before his Death, when I asked him, 'Whether his former Irre-'gularitys were not both accompany'd, at the 'Time, and succeded, afterwards, by some 'Sense of mental Pain?' *Yes,* said he: *but I have scarce ever owned it, 'till now. We* [meaning, We Infidels, and Men of fashionable Morals] *don't tell You all that passes in our Hearts.*

* Prov. xiii. 15. † Prov. xiv. 13.

The *Fact*, then, plainly *is*, that Rectitude of Manners saves People from much Uneasiness of Mind; and, that the Perpetration of moral Evil involves in it a Trojan Horse, whose hidden Force puts their Comforts to the Sword. I have seen Instances of this, in very high, as well as in more humble, Life: notwithstanding all the Labor and Art, which have been obtended, to vail it from the Eye of Man. *They who plough Iniquity, and sow Wickedness, reap the same**: the Crop is always, more or less, similar to the Seed. *The wicked Man travelleth with Pain, all his Days*; and *a dreadfull Sound is in his Ears* †; let him say what he will to the contrary. So that we may almost assert, with ‖ Seneca,

" Prima

---

* Job iv. 8.   † Job xv. 20, 21.

‖ Epist. Lib. 16. Ep. 2.—When St. Paul speaks (Eph. iv. 19.) of some who were ἀπηλγηκότες, which we render, *past Feeling* (tho' it may better be render'd, *quite sunk in Indolence and Idleness*; totally enervated, and dissipated; Enemys to all honest, manly, and laborious Employ:) there is no Necessity for supposing even the English Phrase to import, that those wretched People were void of inward Horror and tormenting Anguish; but that they were quite void of outward Decency, and had no Feelings of Delicacy: for there is a Sort of Refinement (tho' bad is the best), which even Vice itself is capable of.

When the same Apostle speaks, elsewhere (1 *Tim.* iv. 2.), of the κεκαυτηριασμένων, or Persons whose Consciences have been

seared

"Prima & maxima peccantium Pœna est, pec-
"casse:" i. e. *the very Commission of Sin is it's own primary and capital Punishment.*

God Himself has joined the Chain together: no Wonder, therefore, that it's Links cannot be put asunder. Hence, I conclude, that, let what seeming Consequences soever flow from the Position of Necessity; God would not have ty'd moral and natural Evil together, into one Knot, if moral Evil were not justly punishable. And, while FACTS, indisputable FACTS, say, Aye; Facts I will still believe, tho' ten Thousand imaginary *Inferences* were to say, No.

I must likewise add, that, if we shut out the *Doctrine* of Necessity, which asserts the inseparable Connection of moral Evil with intellectual (and, often, with external) Infelicity; Men will want one of the most rational * Motives, which

can

---

seared as with an hot Iron; the Word (not to canvass, here, the several critical Senses which it will admit of) may be fairly consider'd, as importing neither more nor less than This, that they carry a fearfull Brand, or *Mark of Condemnation*, in their own Minds; tho' they may endeavor to toss off Matters, outwardly, with an Air of seeming Unconcern.

* Should Any be so pitiably undiscerning, as to ask, " What can *Necessity* have to do with *rational Motives?*"—I answer: that there are numberless Cases, wherein certain

can possibly induce them to an *Hatred* of Vice. — And so great is the Depravation of Human Nature, that, were it not for the *Thing* Necessity, Virtue neither would nor could have any Sort of Existence in the World.

As for that *Mixture* (or, rather, *Interspersion*) of Good and Evil, which obtains throughout our sublunary Planet; this, likewise, I acknowledge to be the Consequence of actual and reigning Necessity. But this, in a philosophic Eye, reflects no more Blame on Necessity itself; than the two contrary Powers of Attraction and Repulsion can reflect Dishonor on the Wisdom of Him, who, for good Reasons, endu'd Matter with those opposite Propertys.

Motives appear so very *rational* to the Mind, as to be absolutely *cogent*, and incline the Will effectually. For, the finally prædominant *Motive* constantly and infallibly determines the *Will:* and the Will, thus necessarily determin'd, as constantly and infallibly (all extrinsec Impediments removed) determines the Actions of the *Willer*. *Non est Intelligentis Causæ, sine Fine sibi proposito, agere.*

If *Motives* did not so operate on the *Mind*; and if the Mind, so operated upon, did not give Law to the *Will*; and if the Will, so byass'd and conciliated, did not *(positis omnibus ponendis)* necessarily influence the *Conduct*; Actions and Volitions would be uncaused Effects: than which Ideas it is impossible for any Thing to be more absurd and self-contradictory.

Cousin-

Cousin-german to the Second, is Mr. Wesley's 3d. Objection: namely, that, if universal Necessity determine all the Thoughts and Actions of Man, " there can be no Judgement to " come;" i. e. God cannot, in the last Day, judge and sentence Mankind *according* to their Works.—I have, * elsewhere, amply refuted this empty Cavil. But, as it is now hash'd and served up again in a different Dish, I will give it another Examination, before we dismiss it from Table.

The Objector forgets one main Circumstance, of no small Importance to the Argument: viz. that the *Judgement-Day*, itself, and the whole Process of the grand Transaction, together with every Thing that relates to it, directly or indirectly; are, upon the Christian Scheme, no less *necessary* and inevitable, than any intermediate Event can be. An Oak is not more the Daughter of an Acorn; than absolute Necessity will be the Mother of that universal Audit, wherewith she is already pregnant.

But, observe. The *scriptural* is not a *blind* Necessity, or a Necessity resulting (as some of the grosser Stoics believed) either from the planetary Positions, or from the " Stubbornness of Matter." I no where contend for these Kinds of Necessity:

* More Work for Mr. John Wesley, p. 82—85.

which,

which, even admitting them to have their respective Degrees of phyſical Influence, in Subordination to Providence; ſtill can never, by any Chriſtian (nor, I ſhould think, by any Man of refined Underſtanding), be conſider'd as exerciſing the leaſt Dominion over God Himſelf, by inferring any Sort of Cauſality on His interior Purpoſes, or extrinſec Operations.

On the contrary, Neceſſity, in general; with all it's extenſive Series of adamantin Links, in particular; is in reality, what the Poets feigned of Minerva, the Iſſue of Divine Wiſdom: deriving it's whole Exiſtence, from the *Freewill* of God; and it's whole Effectuoſity, from his never-ceaſing *Providence*.

Thus I affirm the Day of Judgement to be *neceſſary:* to-wit, becauſe God has abſolutely * appointed it. For *His Counſel ſhall ſtand, and He will do all His Pleaſure* †. It is alſo NECESSARY, that there ſhould be conſcious Beings, *on whom* to paſs Sentence; and that there ſhould be both good and evil Actions, *on which* the Sentence of the Judge ſhould turn. We muſt, I think, admit this; or, at one Stroke, deny the *certain Futurition* of a Judgement-Day. And, for my own Part, I would much rather believe

---

* Acts xvii. 31.   † Iſaiah xlvi. 10.

and

and maintain so important an Article of revealed Religion, tho' upon the Principle of Necessity; than I would virtually deny it, as an Arminian, by imagining, either the Great *Day* itself, or the *Decisions* of the Day, to be Things of unfixed Chance, lying at sixes and sevens, and which, consequently, may or may not take Effect at all.

'Tis the Doctrine of *uncertain self-Determination*, which, by representing Events to lye at haphazard, stamps Absurdity on the sure Expectation of a Judgement to come. It is the Doctrine of *absolute Necessity*, alone, which, by refusing to hang any one Circumstance on a peradventure, affixes the Seal of infallible Futurity to the Day itself, to the Business of the Day, and to all the Antecedents, Concomitants, and Consequences, of the Whole.

That side-Face of Arminian Freewill, which we have hitherto survey'd, carrys no more than a *squinting* Aspect on the Day of ultimate Retribution; by only leaving the Day, and it's Retributions, at the uncertain Mercy of a *may-be*. Look at the other Profile (i. e. view the *blind* Side) of the Arminian Goddess; and you'll immediately perceive, that, according to HER Scheme of Metaphysics, it is utterly *impossible* there should be any Day of Judgement at all. For,

He

He alone can be called " a *self-determining* " Agent," who is *quite independent* on any other Agent or Agency whatever. If I *depend*, for my Being, for my Ideas, and for my Operations, on Another; my Being, and Ideas, and Operations, are and muſt be *influenced* and affected by that Dependence. Conſequently, I am neither *ſelf-exiſtent* *, nor *ſelf-determined*.—But, if I am an *independent* Animal, I am alſo, neceſſarily, † *ſelf-exiſtent :*

---

* See p. 173. of a Performance already quoted, namely, Dr. *Prieſtley*'s maſterly ' EXAMINATION of Dr. Reid's In- ' quiry into the Human Mind, Dr. Beattie's *Eſſay on Truth*, ' and Dr. Oſwald's *Appeal to Common Senſe*.'—I cannot help obſerving, what, by this Time, almoſt every Perſon knows, and every impartial Judge muſt acknowledge; viz. the Energy and Succeſs, with which Dr. *Prieſtley* has batter'd the Free-will Lanthorns (the *Inquiry*, the *Appeal*, and the *Eſſay*), in which the three Northern Lights had reſpectively ſtuck themſelves and hung themſelves out to public View. It lay, peculiarly, in Dr. *Prieſtley*'s Department, to examine the Theory of thoſe new Lights and Colors. And He has done it to Purpoſe. Tho', I'm apt to think, that the luminous Triumvirate, like Æſop's one-eyed Stag, received the mortal Shot from a Quarter whence they leaſt expected it.

† An *independent Creature* is a Contradiction in Terms. To aſk, " Whether the Deity might not endue created " Beings with philoſophical Independence?" is to aſk, *Whether One God might not make Millions of Others*. I anſwer, No. And yet I do not, by ſo ſaying, " limit the Holy
" One

existent: and I not only may be, but absolutely must be (view what Side of the Argument we will, Necessity stares us in the Face!) I absolutely MUST be a *self-Determinant.* Thus, Self-existence and Independence *necessarily* enter into the Basis of Self-determination, i. e. of Arminian or Methodistical Free-will.

Let us, for a Moment, imagine ourselves to be what Mr. Wesley supposes us.

Lord of myself, is essentially connected with, *Accountable to none.* Farewell, then, to the very Possibility of a Judgement-Day. Shall an *Independent* Being, who can have no Superior, hold up his Hand, as a Felon, at the Bar?—Shall a potent *Self-Exister* deign to be punished, for the evanid Crimes of an Hour?—Shall a sovereign *Self-Determiner* submit to receive Sentence from the Lips of another? Impossible. Paul was a Knave, for asserting it. And Felix was a Fool, for trembling at the empty Sound.

What a truly Christian Tenet, therefore, is that of Free-will! How patly it squares with the Bible! And with how good a grace does *orthodox* Mr. John introduce his

" One of Israel." His Power is still infinite. For, as some have well express'd it, an *essential Contradiction is* NO OBJECT *of Power.*

4th

4th Objection, that "The Scriptures cannot be "of Divine Original," if the Doctrine of Necessity be true.

I, è *contra*, scruple not to declare, that no Man can consistently acknowledge the "Divine "Authority of the Scriptures," without believing their Contents: i. e. without being an absolute Necessitarian. I will even add, that all the intentional Defenders of Christianity in the World, who encounter Deism, or Atheism itself, on any but necessitarian Principles; such Defenders ever will, and inevitably must, have the worst End of the Staff: for the Bible will stand on no Ground but it's own; nor can the Cavillings of it's doctrinal Gainsayers (flimsy as their Cavillings are) be hewn effectually in Pieces, by any Weapons but those which the Bible itself supplys: Among others, it supplys us with the invincible two-edged Sword of *Prædestination* and *Necessity* (which two Edges, by the Way, terminate, Sword-like, in one common * Point): a Weapon, peculiarly

---

* People do not see all Things at once. The Rising of Truth, upon the Mind, is commonly gradual; like the Rising of the Sun, on the World. Hence, some Philosophers, who are rooted *Necessitarians*, either don't yet perceive, or forbear to acknowledge, the Coïncidence of Scripture-Prædestination with physical and metaphysical Necessity.

But,

culiarly formed and temper'd to penetrate the best Mail of our modern unbelieving Philistins; most of whom have Sense enough to laugh (and laugh they may in perfect Safety) at

" *The pointless Arrow and the broken Bow,*"

equipped with which, Arminianism comes limping into the Field of Battle.

But, all in good Time. The more these Doctrines are examin'd, and compared together; the more clearly and strongly will they be found to suppose and support each other. The *Arminians* are aware of this: and pelt both *Prædestination* and *Necessity*, with equal Rage, and with the self-same Cavils.

Nor without Reason. For what is Prædestination, but *Necessitas imperata*; or, the free and everlasting Determination of God, that such and such a Train of Causes and Effects should infallibly take place in Time?—And what is philosophical Necessity, but *Prædestinatio elicita*; or, God's Determination drawn out into Act, by successive Accomplishment, according to the Plan præ-conceived in the Divine Mind?—*Necessity* (i. e. Fate, or Providence, to whose ceaseless Agency all the Laws and Modes and the very Being of Matter and Spirit incessantly subserve) this *Necessity* is, as a valuable Person phrases it, " a strait Line," however crooked it may sometimes appear to us; " a strait " Line, drawn from the Point of God's Decree." And as *Prædestination* is the Point itself, from which the strait Line is drawn; so it is also the Point, into which the Line, progressively, but infallibly, reverts.

The

The *Caput vivum,* of a dextrous Infidel, is absolutely invulnerable by the *Caput mortuum* of Freewill Nonsense, tho' the asinine Jaw-bone were wielded by the Arm of a Samson.

CHAPTER IV.

Specimen of SCRIPTURE-ATTESTATIONS *to the Doctrine of* NECESSITY.

REFERENCES have already been made, in the Course of the present Essay, to several *Scripture* Passages, wherein Necessity is invincibly and decisively asserted. I will add a few others: and then leave the Reader to judge, whether *Necessitarians,* or *Chance-mongers,* give most Credit to the " Divine Original of the " Scriptures."

I witheld thee from sinning against Me. Gen. xx. 6.

It was not You that sent me hither, but God. Gen. l. 5, 7, 8.

I will harden his Heart, that he shall not let the People go. Exod. iv. 21.

It

It was of the Lord, to harden their Hearts, that they should come against Israel to Battle; that He might destroy them utterly. Josh. xi. 20.

The Stars in their Courses fought against Sisera. Judg. v. 20.

The Lord maketh poor, and maketh rich; He bringeth low, and lifteth up. 1 Sam. ii. 7.

They hearkened not to the Voice of their Father; because the Lord would slay them. 1 Sam. ii. 25.

Thus saith the Lord: Behold, I will raise up Evil against thee, out of thy own House; and I will take thy Wives, before thine Eyes, and give them to thy Neighbor, and he shall lie with Wives in the Sight of this Sun.——What was the Consequence?—*So they spread Absalom a Tent upon the Top of the House; and Absalom went in unto his Father's Concubines, in the Sight of all Israel.* 2 Sam. xii. 11. with 2 Sam. xvi. 22.

The Lord hath said unto him [to Shimei], *Curse David.* 2 Sam. xvi. 10.

And he [i. e. the Evil Spirit] *said, I will go forth, and I will be a lying Spirit in the Mouth of all his* [Ahab's] *Prophets. And He* [God] *said, Thou shalt persuade him, and prevail also: go forth, and do so.*—*Now, therefore, the Lord hath put a lying Spirit in the Mouth of all these, &c.* 1 Kings xxii. 22, 23.

Both Riches and Honor come of Thee, and Thou reignest over all. 1 Chron. xxix. 12.

Then rose up the Chief of the Fathers of Judah and Benjamin, &c; whose Spirit God had raised to go up, to build the House of the Lord. Ezra i. 5.

The Lord gave, and the Lord hath taken away. Job i. 21.

Man is born unto Trouble, as the Sparks fly upward (Job v. 7.) And, I'm apt to think, Sparks ascend by *Necessity!*

He disappointeth the Devices of the Crafty, so that their Hands cannot perform their Enterprize. (Job v. 12.) Be Men ever so shrewd, their utmost Dexterity will not avail, unless the Great Superintending Creator stamp it with Efficiency.

Behold, He taketh away. Who can hinder Him? Who will say unto Him [i. e. who has a *Right* to say unto God], *What dost thou?* Job ix. 12.—*For He is not a Man, as I am, that I should answer Him, and that we should come together in Judgement.* Ver. 32.

Vain Man would be wise [and the puny Prisoner of a Clod would be an independent, self-determining Freewiller!], *tho' Man be born as a wild Ass's Colt.* Job xi. 12.—What a Thunderbolt to human Pride! To the το αυτεξusιον. To αυτοδεσποτια. To the τα εφ' ημιν. To αυτοκρατορια. To

To *Liberum Arbitrium*. To *Ipseitas*. To the Arminian Herb called, *Self-heal*. To *Independency, Self-Authority, Self-determination, Self-Salvation, innate Ideas*, and other pompous Nothings, with which Man's Ignorance and Conceit seek to plat a Wreath for the Enrichment of his Brows. *Vain Man, born as a wild Ass's* * Colt!*
" How

* And we should *remain*, to our dying Day, nearly on a Level with the Animal to which we are compared, were it not for the Care of those about us, and did we not *necessarily* become Parts of a Society antecedently formed to our Hands. In what a State would the present Generation be, had they not dropt (if I may use the Expression) into an House ready built! i. e. if we had been cut off from all Means of profiting by the Wisdom, the Experience, the Discoverys, the Inventions, and the Regulations, of those who lived before us. 'Tis a Circumstance of unspeakable Convenience, to be the Children of Time's Old Age.

Our mental Powers, like Chicken in their Shell, or a Plant in it's Semen, are no more than virtual and dormant, 'till elicited by Cultivation, and ripen'd by Experience, Attention, and Reflection. Civil Society, Dress, articulate Language, with all other usefull and ornamental Polishings which result from domestic and political Connection, are, in themselves, Things purely *artificial* and adventitious. If so, will it not follow, that (ever since the Fall) Man is, naturally, a wild Animal? Some very able Reasoners have gone so far, as peremptorily to pronounce him such. The late Dr. *Young*, in his " Centaur not fabulous," appears to have thought, that the greater Part of the Human Species profit so little by their accessory Opportunitys of Improvement,

E 2

"How keenly," says a fine Writer, " is this
" Comparison pointed! — Like the *Ass's:* an
" Animal,

ment, as to go off the Stage, Semi Savages, at last; notwithstanding the inexhaustible and omnipotent Deluge of FREE-WILL, which that ingenious Writer imagined every Man to bring into the World with him. Strange, that so immense a Reservoir, inhærent in the Soul, should yet leave the Soul so dry!

With Regard to the natural Wildness of Man, supposed and asserted by some Philosophers; thus much, I think, must be fairly admitted: that the Hypothesis derives much subsidiary Force, from various pertinent and well-authenticated *Facts*. For, if any Credit be due to human Testimony, there have been Instances of exposed Infants, who were nursed by Forest Animals; and, when grown up, went prone on all-four, with a Swiftness greatly superior to that of the nimblest Running-Footman: but totally unable (and no Wonder) to form the least articulate Sound. 'Tis added, that, like any other wild Creature, they would fly from the human Sight (i. e. from the Sight of their own Species *refined)*, with a Roar of Fear and Hatred, into the thickest Recesses of the Woods.

Civilization, tho' a very poor Succedaneum for that Divine Image, originally impress'd on our immortal Part, and lost by Adam's Transgression; is, however, of very great sæcular Importance. Nay, it's Importance is, with Regard to Millions of us, more than sæcular: for it is often a Providential Means of qualifying us to receive and understand that blessed Gospel, which, when made the Vehicle of Divine Power to the Heart, issues in our Recovery of God's Image, and in the Salvation of the Soul.

After

"Animal, remarkable for it's Stupidity, even
"to a Proverb.—Like the Aſs's *Colt:* which
"muſt be ſtill more egregiouſly ſtupid than the
"Dam.—Like the *wild* Aſs's Colt: which is
"not only blockiſh, but ſtubborn and intract-
"able; neither poſſeſſes valuable Qualitys by
"Nature, nor will eaſily receive them by Diſ-
"cipline.—The Image, in the Original, is yet
"more ſtrongly touched. The comparative
"Particle *like*, is not in the Hebrew. *Born a*
"*wild Aſs's Colt.* Or, as we ſhould ſay in
"Engliſh, *A mere wild*, &c." (HERVEY's
Theron and Aſpaſio, Dial. 13.)

He [i. e. God] *is in one Mind, and who can turn Him? and what His Soul deſireth, even That He doth. He performeth the Thing that is appointed for me. And many ſuch Things are with Him.* Job xxiii. 13, 14.—Quæry: Who is *Self-*

After all, let the Inſtruments of our Refinement, and of our Knowledge (whether in Things temporal, or in Things ſacred), be Who or What they may; and let us profit ever ſo deeply by our Intercourſe with the living, by Converſe with the recorded Wiſdom of the dead, by the Perceptions we receive from external Objects, and by Reflecting on the Ideas of which thoſe Perceptions are the Source: Still, no Advantages are any Thing more to us, than Divine Providence makes them to be. *Let him, therefore, that glorys, glory in the Lord.* For, it is God, *who teacheth Us more than the Beaſts of the Earth, and maketh Us wiſer than the Fowls of Heaven.* 1 Cor. i. 31. Job xxxv. 11.

Determiner?

Determiner? Man, or God? Surely, God. Nor is He only the Self-Determiner, but the *All-Determiner* likewife; throughout the whole Univerfe both of Spirits and of Matter.

For He looketh to the Ends of the Earth, and feeth under the whole Heaven: To make a Weight for the Winds; and He weigheth the Waters by Meafure. He made a Decree for the Rain, and a Way for the Lightening of the Thunder. Job xxviii. 25, 26.

When He giveth Quietnefs, who then can make Trouble? and, when He hideth His Face, who then can behold Him? whether it be done againft a Nation, or againft a Man only. Job xxxiv. 29.— Abfolute *Neceffity* ftill.

By the Breath of God, Froft is given: and the Breadth of the Waters is ftraiten'd. Alfo, by Watering, He wearieth the thick Cloud: He fcattereth His bright Cloud. He caufeth it to come: whether for Correction, or for His Land, or for Mercy. Job xxxviii. 10—13.—We fee, from this, as well as from a præceding and from two or three fubfequent Quotations, that the Air cannot be compreffed into a Current of *Wind*; nor *Rain* find it's Way to the Earth; nor Exhalations kindle into *Thunder* and *Lightening*; nor a *River* overflow it's Banks; nor fufpended Vapors condenfe into *Snow* or *Hail*; nor Water *freeze*, or, when

when frozen, *thaw*; without the expreſs Appointment of God's Will, and the Hand of His particular Providence. Second Cauſes are but Effects of His Decree: and can operate no farther, than He, from whom they derive their whole Activity, condeſcends to make Uſe of them as Mediums of His own Agency.

The Kingdom is the Lord's: and He is the Governor among the Nations. Pſalm xxii. 28.

O Lord, Thou preſerveſt Man and Beaſt. Pſalm xxxvi. 6.

Except the Lord build the Houſe, they labor in vain that build it. Except the Lord keep the City, the Watchman waketh but in vain. Pſalm cxxvii. 1.

Whatſoever the Lord pleaſed, that did He; in Heaven, and in Earth, in the Seas, and in all deep Places. He cauſeth the Vapors to aſcend from the Ends of the Earth: He maketh Lightenings, for the Rain: He bringeth the Wind out of His Treaſurys. Pſalm cxxxv. 6, 7.

He covereth the Heaven with Clouds, He prepareth Rain for the Earth, He maketh Graſs to grow upon the Mountains. He giveth to the Beaſt his Food; and to the young Ravens, which cry.——He maketh Peace in thy Borders, and filleth thee with the fineſt Wheat.—He giveth Snow, like Wool; He ſcattereth the Hoar Froſt, like Aſhes.

He casteth forth His Ice, like Morsels: who can stand before His Cold? He sendeth out His Word, and melteth them: He causeth His Wind to blow, and the Waters flow. Psalm cxlvii. 8, 9, 14—18. — What so variable and uncertain, humanly speaking, as the *Weather?* And yet, we see, all it's Modes and Changes are adjusted and determined, from Moment to Moment, by Divine Impression: i. e. by a *Necessity*, resulting from the Will and Providence of the Supreme First Cause. *Fire, and Hail; Snow, and Vapor; Stormy Wind; fullfilling His Word!* Psalm cxlviii. 8.

Neither is *material* Nature alone thus " * *bound* " *fast in Fate.*" All other Things, the " *Hu-* " *man Will*" itself not excepted, are no less tightly bound, i. e. effectually influenced and determined. For,

The Preparations of the Heart, in Man; and the Answer of the Tongue; are from the Lord. Prov. xvi. 1. That is, Men can neither *think*, nor *speak*; they can neither *resolve*, nor *act*; independently of Providence.

The Lord hath made all Things, for Himself; for the Manifestation of His own Glory, and for the Accomplishment of His own Designs: *even*

---

* See *Pope*'s Universal Prayer.

the Wicked, for the Day of Evil. Prov. xvi. 4.— If so, He has endued none of His Creatures with a *Self-determining* Power, which might issue in Counter-acting and Defeating the Purposes of His infinite Wisdom.

A Man's Heart deviseth his Way: but the Lord directeth his Steps. Prov. xvi. 9.——Yea, *There are many Devices in a Man's Heart: nevertheless; the Counsel of the Lord,* THAT *shall stand.* Prov. xix. 21.

The Lot is cast into the Lap: but the whole Disposing thereof is of the Lord. Prov. xvi. 33.

Even *the King's Heart is in the Hand of the Lord, as the Rivers of Water: and He turneth it, whithersoever He will.* Prov. xxi. 1.—Odd Sort of *Self-Determination,* this!

Enemys, and evil-minded Men, are under the absolute Controll of God; nor can their Enmity, or their Wickedness, do a Jot more Hurt, than He gives Leave.—*O Assyrian, the Rod of* MY *Anger.* Isai. x. 5.—*Thou art* MY *Battle-axe and Weapons of War: for with thee will I break in Pieces the Nations, and with thee will I destroy Kingdoms.* Jer. li. 20.—Very extraordinary Declarations these, if Men are *Self-determining* Agents! a Self-determining *Rod,* for Instance: a Self-determining *Battle-Axe:* a Self-determining *Hammer!* Arminianism does That, which

God,

God, by the Prophet, satirizes in the following lively Terms: *Shall the* AXE *boast itself against Him that heweth therewith? or shall a* SAW *magnify itself against Him that shaketh it? As if the* ROD *should shake itself against Them that lifted up! or, as if* A STAFF *should lift up itself as though it were no Wood!* Isai. x. 15.—What! is that noble Free-willer, MAN, comparable to an *Axe*, to a *Saw*, to a *Rod*, and to a *Stick*; not one of which can operate, or so much as move, but in Proportion as 'tis acted upon? This is worse than being likened to Mr. Wesley's *Clock-work!* But who can help it?

The Prophet goes on, elsewhere. *The Lord of Hosts hath sworn* [i. e. hath solemnly and immutably decreed], *saying, Surely, as I have thought, so shall it come to pass: and as I have purposed, so shall it stand.—This is the Purpose, which is purposed upon the whole Earth; and this is the Hand that is stretched out upon all the Nations. For the Lord of Hosts hath purposed, and who shall disannull it? And His Hand is stretched out, and who shall turn it back?* Isai. xv. 24, 26, 27.—Grand and conclusive Quæstions! Quæstions, however, which lordly Arminianism can solve in a Moment. *Who shall dis-annull God's Purpose?* Why, human *Freewill* to be sure.—*Who shall turn back God's Hand?* Human *Self-determination* can do it, with as much Eafe as our Breath can repel the Down of a Feather!

I form the Light, and create Darknefs: I make Peace, and create Evil. I the Lord do all thefe Things. Ifai. xlv. 7.

Who is he that faith, and it cometh to pafs; when the Lord commandeth it not? Lam. iii. 37. The higheft Angel cannot.

Wifdom and Might are God's. *He changeth the Times and the Seafons. He removeth Kings, and fetteth up Kings. He giveth Wifdom to the Wife, and Knowledge to them that know Underftanding.* Dan. ii. 20, 21.

Locufts, and other ravaging Infects, cannot afflict a Land, without a Commiffion under the Great Seal of Providence. *The Locuft, the Canker-worm, the Caterpillar, and the Palmer-worm; my great Army, which I fent among you.* Joel ii. 25.

Shall there be Evil in a City [viz. any *Calamitous Accident*, as 'tis commonly called], *and the Lord hath not done it?* Amos iii. 6.—Impoffible.

I caufed it to rain upon one City, and caufed it not to rain upon another City.—I have fmitten You with Blafting, and Mildew.—I have fent among You the Peftilence.—Your young Men have I flain with the Sword. Amos iv. 7—10.

They

They [Paul and Timothy] *were forbidden of the Holy Ghoſt to preach the Word in Aſia.*—*They eſſayed to go into Bithynia: but the Spirit ſuffer'd them not.* Acts. xvi. 6, 7. Had Self-determination any Thing to do here?

A certain Woman, named Lydia, heard us: whoſe Heart the Lord opened, ſo that ſhe attended to the Things that were ſpoken by Paul. Ibid. ⅴ. 14.

As many, as were ordained unto eternal Life, believed. Acts xiii. 48.

I am carnal, ſold under Sin. For that which I do, ꙋ γινωσκω, *I am far from approving: for what I would, that do I not; but what I hate, that do I.*——*To will is preſent with me: but how to perform that which is good, I find not. For the Good that I would, I do not: but the Evil which I would not, that I do.*——*When I would do Good, Evil is preſent with me. I delight in the Law of God, after the inner Man: but I ſee another Law in my Members, warring againſt the Law of my Mind, and bringing me into Captivity to the Law of Sin which is in my Members. O wretched Man that I am! Who ſhall deliver me from the Body of this Death? I thank God, through Jeſus Chriſt our Lord. So then, with the Mind, I myſelf ſerve the Law of God: but, with my Fleſh, the Law of Sin.* Rom. vii. 14—25. According to the Account which St. Paul here gives of himſelf, he no more dreamed

of

of his being a *Self-determiner*, than of his having attained to *finless Perfection*. No Wonder that some flaming Arminians have a peculiar Spite against this Apostle!

In Whom [i. e. in Christ] *we also have obtained an Inheritance : being* PRÆDESTINATED, *according to the Purpose of Him who* WORKETH ALL THINGS ACCORDING TO THE COUNSEL OF HIS OWN WILL. Eph. i. 11.

Speaking of *Affliction* and Persecution, the Apostle comforted himself and his fellow-sufferers, by resolving All into Necessity : *That no Man should be moved by these Afflictions ; for Ye yourselves know, that we are* APPOINTED *thereto.* 1 Thess. iii. 3.

What Idea St. *James* entertained, concerning Freewill and Self-determination, fully appears from the following Admonition : *Ye know not* [much less can ye be the Disposers of] *what shall be on the Morrow. For what is your Life ? it is even a Vapor that appeareth for a little Time, and then vanisheth away. Ye ought to say,* IF THE LORD WILL, *we shall live, and do this, or that.* James iv. 14, 15.—Why did St. James reason in this Manner ? Because he was endued with Grace and Sense to be a *Necessitarian*.

So was St. *Peter*. Hence he tells the Regenerated Elect, to whom he wrote, *Ye also, as*

lively

lively Stones, are built up, a spiritual House. 1 Pet. ii. 5. This is giving Freewill a Stab under the fifth Rib. For, can *Stones* hew themselves, and *build* themselves into a regular *House?* no more, in this Apostle's Judgement, can Men form themselves into Temples of the Holy Ghost. It is the Effect of *necessitating* Grace.

The Prophecy came not, in old Time, by the Will of Man: but holy Men of God spake as they were moved by the Holy Ghost. 2 Pet. i. 21.—Necessity, again.

There shall come, in the last Days, Scoffers, walking after their own Lusts. 2 Pet. iii. 3.—But the Apostle could not have been sure of this, without taking *Necessity* into the Account: or, as himself expresses it, unless they, who *stumble at the Word,* were APPOINTED *to Disobedience.* 1 Pet. ii. 8.

There are certain Men crept in unawares, who were, BEFORE, *of old,* ORDAINED *to this Condemnation.* Jude 4. If so, were not the Sin and Condemnation of those Men *necessary* and inevitable?

CHAP.

CHAPTER V.

Proofs that CHRIST *Himself was an absolute* NECESSITARIAN.

LEST any, who may not, hitherto, have considered the Subject, with the same Attention that I have done, should be startled at the Title of this Chapter; I shall adduce the larger Evidence, in Order to make good what the Title imports. The Reader will not, however, expect a Synopsis of the *whole* Evidence, by which this great Truth is authenticated: for, were I to attempt *that*, I must transcribe well-nigh all the 89 Chapters of the four Evangelists.

It should seem, that our Blessed Lord began His public Ministrations with His Sermon on the Mount, recorded *Matt.* V. VI. and VII. In that Discourse, are the following Passages.

One Jot, or one Tittle, shall in no wise pass from the Law, 'till all be fullfilled.

Thou canst not make one Hair white or black.

Your Father, who is in Heaven, maketh His Sun to rise on the evil and the good, and sendeth Rain on the just and on the unjust. Surely, Man can neither promote, nor hinder, the Rising of the Sun and the Falling of the Rain!

Thine *is the Kingdom, and the Power, and the Glory, for ever.*—How can a Free-willer say the Lord's Prayer?

Which of you, by taking Thought, can add one Cubit unto his Stature? The Word ἡλικια signifys both *Stature,* and *Age.* As we have no single Term, in English, which comprizes both those Ideas together; the Passage should be render'd periphrastically: *Which of you, by being anxious, can either make Addition to his Stature, or prolong the Duration of his Life?*

Be not tormentingly distressed, concerning Futurity: for Futurity shall take Care of it's own Things. Sufficient unto the Day is the Evil thereof: i. e. Commit yourselves, in a believing and placid Use of reasonable Means, to the Will and Providence of Him, who has already lain out the whole Plan of Events in His own immutable Purpose. The appointed Measure of supposed *Evil* is infallibly connected with it's *Day:* which no Corrodings of imaginary Anticipation can either stave off, or diminish.

" Reasonable *Means!* are not all Means, hereby, shut out of the Case?" No. Not in any Respect whatever. For we know not what Means God will bless, 'till we have try'd as many as we can.

can. But, when all tryed, the Refult ftill refts with Him.

I fhall only quote one other Paffage, from the Sermon on the Mount.—*The Rain* [of Affliction] *defcended, and the Floods* [of Temptation] *came, and the Winds* [of Perfecution] *blew, and beat upon that Houfe* [the Houfe of an Elect, Redeemed, Converted Soul]: *but it fell not; for it was founded upon a Rock.* That is, in plain Englifh, it *could not* fall. It ftood, *neceffarily:* or, as the Senfe is yet more forcibly exprefs'd in St. Luke, *When the Flood arofe, the Stream beat vehemently upon that Houfe, and* COULD NOT *fhake it.* Luke vi. 48.

In other Parts of the Gofpels, we find CHRIST reafoning and acting on the higheft Principles of abfolute Neceffity.

I will; *Be thou clean:* faid He, to the poor Leper. What was the Confequence? *And immediately his Leprofy was cleanfed.* Matt. viii. 3.—The effect *neceffarily* followed. The Leper *could not but* be healed.

And, indeed, what were all the *Miracles* wrought by JESUS, but Effects of His *irrefiftible* and *neceffitating* Power? Let the Chriftian Reader examine and weigh each of thofe Miracles, with this Remark in his Eye; and he will foon become a Convert to the Doctrine of Neceffity.

F   Was

Was it possible for those Miracles *not* to have taken Effect? i. e. was it possible for Christ's Miracles *not* to have been Miracles? Was it *Chance*, which armed His Word with Ability to heal and to destroy? If so, farewell to all Christianity at once. I can perceive no Shadow of Medium between *Necessity* and rank *Infidelity*.

Neither can I make any Thing of the *Prophecys* of Christ, unless those Prophecys be considered as *infallible:* i. e. as inferring a *certain*, or *necessary*, Accomplishment, in every Part. For, if a single prædicted Circumstance *can possibly* happen, *otherwise* than it is foretold; the entire Argument, for the Truth of Divine Revelation, drawn from the Topic of Prophecy, moulders into Dust.

Nor is the Arminian *Self-determining* Hypothesis more compatible with (what is the essential Basis of Prophecy) the *Fore-Knowledge* of God. If, for Example, it so lay at the Freewill of Christ's Betrayer and Murderers, that they *might*, or might *not*, have betrayed and crucify'd Him; and if it so lay at the Freewill of the Romans, as that they *might*, or might *not*, have destroyed Jerusalem; it will follow, that those Events were philosophically *contingent:* i. e. there was *no Certainty* of their taking place, till after they *actually had* taken place. The Self-determining Will of
Judas

Judas *might possibly* have determined itself another Way. So *might* the Self-determining Will of every Person concerned in the Crucifixion of Christ. And so *might* the Self-determining Wills of those Romans, who besieged and raz'd Jerusalem. Consequently (on that Principle,) Divine *Foreknowledge* could not, *with Certainty*, know any Thing of the Matter. For that which is *not certainly future*, is not *certainly foreknowable*. It may be emptily consider'd, as *possible*: or (at the very utmost) be uncertainly guessed at, as *not improbable*. But KNOWLEDGE must be left quite out of the Quæstion: for *Knowledge* will stand on *none but* * CERTAIN *Ground*. God does

not

---

* There are four Links, which all the Art of Man can never separate; and which procede in the following order: *Decree — Foreknowledge — Prophecy — Necessity*. Let us take a short Scripture View of these sacred Links, and of their Connection with each other.

I am GOD, *and there is none else*; *I am* GOD, *and there is none like Me*: DECLARING *the End, from the Beginning; and, from antient Times, the Things that are not yet done: saying,* MY COUNSEL SHALL STAND, AND I WILL DO ALL MY PLEASURE. — — — *Yea, I have spoken: I will also bring it to pass. I have* PURPOSED: *I will also* DO *it*. Isaiah xlvi. 9, 10, 11. I admit, that this sublime Passage had *immediate* Reference to the certainty of Babylon's Capture by Cyrus. But not to That *only*. " The THINGS *which are* " *not yet done*," as well as That in particular, are, *all*, known not *fore*-know, but *after*-know (i. e. He is never *sure* of a Thing's coming to pass, 'till it *does* or has

to Jehovah; and *many* of 'em explicitly prædicted likewise. And on what is God's absolute and all-comprizing Knowledge *grounded?* On the " COUNSEL", or Decree; and on the " PLEASURE", or sovereign and almighty Determination; of His WILL.—By the same Rule, that God had *prædestinated*, and did *foreknow*, the Exploits of Cyrus; He must have prædestinated, and foreknown, the Exploits of every other Man. Since, if any ONE Being, or any ONE Fact, Incident, or Circumstance, be *unknown* to God; EVERY Being, Fact, Incident, and Circumstance, may be equally unknown by Him. But, putting Matters upon the best Footing on which Arminianism can put them; the *Divine Knowledge* can neither be *eternal*, nor *infinite*, nor *infallible*, if aught is exempted from it, or if aught can happen otherwise than as it is foreknown.

How great a Stress God lays, on this His Attribute of complete and unmistaking PRÆSCIENCE; and how He claims the Honor of it, as one of those essential and incommunicable Perfections, by which He stands distinguished from false gods; may be seen, among other places, in *Isaiah* XLI. 21, 22, 23. and XLII. 8, 9. and XLIII. 9, 12. and XLV. 21.—Well, therefore, might St. James declare, in the Synod of Apostles and Elders held at Jerusalem, *Known unto* GOD *are All his Works*, απ' αιων⊙, *from Eternity.* Acts xv. 18.

The late excellent Mr. *William Cooper*, of Bolton, in New-England, (I say, the late; because I suppose that good man to be, e'er this Time, gathered into the Assembly of Saints made perfect); observes, in the Second of his *Four Discourses on Prædestination unto Life*, that it was the Scripture Doctrine
of

has come to pass), if it be in the Power of His Creatures to determine themselves to a contrary Point of the Compass.

" Oh, but God foreknows to what particular " Point of the Compass they *certainly will* de- " termine themselves." Pray, leave out the Word, *certainly*; and likewise the Word, *will:* for they stab poor *Self-determination* to the Heart. If you retain those Words and their Ideas, you give up the very Essence of your Cause. For, what *certainly will* be, is no longer *uncertain.*

of God's OMNISCIENCE, which proselyted our famous Dr.
South to Calvinism. " I have it," says Mr. Cooper, " from
" very good Authority" [appealing, in the Margin, to Dr.
Calamy's Continuation, Vol. I. p. 146.], " that, some
" Time after the Restoration, Dr. *South* being in Company,
" at Oxford, with several Persons of Note, and among the
" Rest with Mr. *Thomas Gilbert*, who was afterwards one of
" the ejected Ministers; they fell into a Conversation, about
" the *Arminian* Points. —— On Mr. Gilbert's asserting, that
" the PRÆDESTINATION, *of the Calvinists, did necessarily*
" *follow upon the* PRÆSCIENCE *of the Arminians;* the Doctor
" presently engaged, that, *If he* [Gilbert] *could make That*
" *out, he* [i. e. Dr. South] *would never be an Arminian, so*
" *long as he lived.* Mr. Gilbert immediately undertook it:
" and made good his Assertion, to the Satisfaction of those
" present. And the Doctor himself was so convinced, as to
" continue, to the last, a very zealous Assertor of the Re-
" formed [i. e. of the Calvinistic] Doctrine, against it's
" various Opposers."

And what is *not uncertain* is NECESSARY, or *will surely* come to pass, and *cannot but* do so: elfe, the *Certainty* evaporates into nothing.

When Chrift fent his Difciples for an Afs's Colt, which, He foreknew and foretold, they would find exactly at fuch a Place; He added, that the Owner of the Animal, on their faying, *The Lord wants it*, would immediately permit them to lead it away. They went to the Village, and made up to the very Spot; where every Thing fell out, præcifely, as their Heavenly Mafter had prædicted. Let me afk: Was the Man's *Confent* to part with his Colt *neceffary*; or was it *uncertain?* All Circumftances confider'd, had he Power to *refufe*, and might he *actually* have refufed to let go his Property? If (which was certainly the Cafe) he *could not poffibly* withhold his Affent, Chrift's *Foreknowledge* was real; and the Man himfelf, what the ingenious Mr. Wefley would term, "a fine Piece of Clock-work;" but what I fhould term, a *neceffary Free-Agent*. If, on the other Hand, he *might* have denied complying with the Difciples' Requeft, and *could poffibly* have difmiffed them without Succefs: it will *neceffarily* follow, that our Lord fhot His Arrow at a venture, fent His Meffengers on a blind Errand, and that His own Foreknowledge was *not* Foreknowledge, but random Conjecture

and

and Surmize. — " Oh, but our Lord foreknew " that the Man *certainly would* do as requefted." Then the Man *could not help* doing it. His Volition was *inevitable*. It could not have been *infallibly known*, that he *certainly would* comply; if that Compliance was antecedently *uncertain*, and if it *could* fo have happen'd that he might *not* have comply'd.

Thus does SCRIPTURE-PROPHECY (not one only, but every individual Prophecy in God's Book) demonftrate, 1. The abfolute *Foreknowledge* of the Three Divine Perfons: and, 2. The unalterable *Neceffity*, or indefeatable Futurition, of Things foreknown.

Either God is *ignorant* of future Events, and his Underftanding, like that of Men, receives gradual *Improvement* from Time and Experience and Obfervation (a Suppofition blacker, if poffible, than Atheifm itfelf!); or, the whole Train of Incidents, even to the Rife and Fall of a Mote in the Air, ever *was*, now *is*, ever *will* be, and ever *muft* be, exactly That, and no other, which He * *certainly knew* it would be. FORE-KNOW-

LEDGE,

---

* Properly fpeaking, it cannot be affirmed of God, that He either *did* know, or that He *will* know; but, fimply, that He *knows*. For, *In Deum non cadunt prius & pofterius:* there is no *paft*, nor *future*, to HIM. All is *prefent*, and unfucceffive.

LEDGE, undarkened by the leaſt Shadow of *Ignorance*, and ſuperior to all Poſſibility of *Miſtake*;

unſucceſſive. The Diſtribution of Things, into thoſe that *have* been, thoſe that *are*, and thoſe that *ſhall* be; is, indeed, ſuited to the flux Condition, and to the limited Facultys, of Beings like ourſelves, whoſe Eſtimates of Duration are taken from the periodical Journeys of an apaque Grain, round lucid Speck termed the Sun: but can have no Place in Him, of whom it is declared, that *a Thouſand Years are, with the* LORD, *as one Day; and one Day, as a Thouſand Years*. And even this Declaration, magnificent as it is, falls *infinitely* ſhort of the Mark.

When, therefore, I ſpeak of *Foreknowledge*, as an Attribute eſſential to Deity; I ſpeak, as St. Paul ſays, *after the Manner of Men*. The ſimple Term, *Knowledge*, would be more intrinſecally proper: but then it would not ſo readily aid the Conceptions of ordinary Perſons. Though, for my own Part, I would, always, rather call the Divine Knowledge, *Omniſcience*, than give it any other Name.

Let me juſt hint, that, if *all Things*, without Exception, and without Succeſſion, are eternally *preſent*, as an indiviſible Point, to the Uncreated View; NECESSITY comes in, with a full Tide. For that, which is always a philoſophical NOW, can be no other, nor otherwiſe, than it *is*.—Not to add: that the Deity, whoſe View of all Things is thus unchangeably fixed, and perpetual, and intranſitory; muſt have within Himſelf a conſtant and irremediable ſource of ſtanding *Uneaſineſs*, if any Thing can happen in Contrariety to his Will, and ſo as to croſs or defeat the Wiſdom and Goodneſs of his Deſigns. He muſt certainly intereſt Himſelf, and very deeply too, in the Accompliſhment of a Will which is

all-holy,

Mistake; is a Link, which draws invincible NECESSITY after it, whether the Scripture Doctrine of Prædestination be taken into the Account or no.

Take a few more Evidences of our Lord's Necessitarianism.

When they deliver you up [to be try'd as religious Criminals at the Jewish and Heathen Tribunals], *take no Thought how or what ye shall speak. For it shall be* GIVEN *you, in that same Hour, what ye shall speak. For it is not ye that speak, but the Spirit of your Father, who speaketh in you.* Matt. x. 19, 20.

Are not two Sparrows sold for a Farthing? and one of them shall not fall on the Ground, without your Father. But the very HAIRS *of your Head are all numbered.* Matt. x. 29, 30.

O Father, THOU *hast* HID *these Things from the wise and prudent, and hast* REVEALED *them unto Babes.* Matt. xi. 25.

It is GIVEN *unto You, to know the Mysterys of the Kingdom of Heaven: but to them it is* NOT *given.* Matt. xiii. 11.

all-holy, and all-right, and all-wise. Consequently, could *such* a Will (and his Will is præcisely such) be frustrated, though but in one single Instance; that Frustration would necessarily be a *Calamity* on God Himself, and inflict essential and never-ending *Pain* on the Divine Mind. Another (I think, irrefragable) Proof, that nothing is left to Contingency.

Without

Without a Parable spake He not unto them: that it might be FULLFILLED, *which was spoken by the Prophet.* Matt. xiii. 34, 35.

Flesh and Blood have not revealed this unto thee, but my FATHER *who is in Heaven.* Matt. xvi. 17.

Upon this Rock WILL *I build my Church, and the Gates of Hell* SHALL NOT *prevail against it.* Ver. 18.

The Son of Man MUST *go to Jerusalem, and suffer many Things, and be killed, and rise again the third Day.* Ver. 21.

It MUST NEEDS *be* [Αναἴκη εϛι, *there is a* NECESSITY] *that Offences come.* Matt. xviii. 7.— Or, as St. Luke has it, *It is* IMPOSSIBLE [ανενδεκτον, *it is not expectable*] *but that Offences will come:* Luke xvii. 1. Our Lord not only afserted the *Thing*, which we mean by NECESSITY; but even made Use of the *Word* itself. And so we find Him doing, in three or four other Parts of the Gospels. Nor is the Sense, in which He used the Term, left ambiguous: as appears from comparing the two above Passages together. *Necessity* is that, by which, Things *cannot*, without the utmost Folly and Absurdity, *be expected* to come to pass *any otherwise* than just as they do. But Arminianism pays very slender Regard to Christ's Authority.

Go

Go thou to the Sea, and caſt an Hook, and take the Fiſh that firſt cometh up: and, when thou haſt open'd his Mouth, thou ſhalt find a Piece of Money. Matt. xvii. 27.

All Men CANNOT *receive this Saying, ſave they to whom it is given. He that* CAN *receive it, let him receive it.* Matt. xix. 11, 12.

To ſit on my right Hand and on my left, is not mine to give, except unto THEM *for whom it is prepared of my Father.* Matt. xx. 23.

Let no Fruit grow on thee henceforward, forever. And, preſently, the Fig-tree wither'd away. Matt. xxi. 19.

Whoſoever ſhall fall on this Stone, ſhall be broken: but on whomſoever it ſhall fall, it will grind him to Powder. Matt. xxi. 44.

Many are called, but few are choſen. Matt. xxii. 14.

Fill ye up the Meaſure of your Fathers.——— *How* * CAN *Ye eſcape the Damnation of Hell?* Matt. xxiii. 32, 33.

I ſend

---

* Monſieur *Le Clerc* (who would have thought it?) has a Paſſage, ſo full to the Senſe of this obſervable Text, that one would almoſt imagine he deſigned it for the very Purpoſe. " Poſito, Hominem Peccato deditum eſſe; nec per
" totam Vitam id habere, quod *neceſſariò* poſtulatur ad Ha-
" bitum Peccati exuendum; inde colligimus, *Neceſſitate*
" *Conſequentiæ,* Hominem in Peccato MANSURUM, nec ullâ
" Ratione

I send unto you Prophets, and wise Men, and Scribes: and some of them ye SHALL *kill and crucify; and some of them* SHALL *ye scourge in your Synagogues; and persecute them from City to City; that upon* YOU *may come all the righteous Bloodshed upon the Earth.* Matt. xxiii. 34, 35.— Say not, " Where is the " Justice of this?" Justice belongs to another

" Ratione vitaturum *Pœnas* Peccatori *debitas* impænitenti." Ontolog. Cap. 13.

I really *wonder*, at the above Writer's expressing himself thus. But *I do* NOT *wonder*, to hear the excellent LUTHER remark as follows. " Nonne clarè sequitur, dum Deus " Opere suo in nobis non adest, omnia esse MALA quæ " facimus, et nos NECESSARIÒ operari quæ nihil ad Salutem " valent? Si enim non nos, sed solus Deus operatur Salutem " in nobis; nihil, ante Opus ejus, operamur salutare, " velimus nolimus." (De *Servo Arbitr.* Sect. 43.) i. e. *It is clearly evident, that, 'till God is present in us by His own gracious Influence,* WHATEVER *we do is* EVIL*: and we* NECESSARILY *do those Things only, which have no Tendency to Salvation. For if it is God alone who worketh Salvation in Us, and not We in Ourselves; we can do nothing salutary, will we or nill we, 'till He Himself actually doth so work in us.* — Well said, honest *Martin.* To God's Blessing upon the bold and faithfull Assertion of such noble Truths as This, we owe our REFORMATION from Popery. And nothing will finally preserve us from being carryed captive into the Popish Egypt again, but the Revival and Prævalency of the same noble Truths which at first led us forth from that House of Bondage.

Argument.

Argument. We are not now treating of *Justice*, but of *Necessity*. Keep to the Point.

Two Men shall be in the Field: ONE *shall be taken, and the* OTHER *left. Two Women shall be grinding at the Mill: one shall be taken and the other left.* Matt. xxiv. 40, 41.

This Night, before the Cock crow, thou SHALT DENY *me thrice.* Matt. xxvi. 34. — Might Peter *not* have deny'd Him? and might Christ have proved *mistaken?*

If it be POSSIBLE, *let this Cup pass from me.* Matt. xxvi. 39. — But it was *not* possible.

Thinkest thou that I cannot now pray to my Father, &c; *but how then shall the Scriptures be fullfilled, that thus it* MUST *be?* Ver. 53, 54.

All this was done, THAT *the Scriptures of the Prophets might be fullfilled.* Ver. 56.

And they crucifyed Him, and parted His Garments, casting Lots; that it MIGHT *be* FULLFILLED *which was spoken,* &c. Matt. xxvii. 35.—Nothing but shere Necessity, from Beginning to End!

My Appeals to the other Three Evangelists shall be extremely concise.

He goeth up into a Mountain, and calleth unto Him whom He WOULD *and they* * CAME *unto Him.* Mark iii. 13. *If*

---

* It is præcisely the same, in the spiritual *Conversion* of the Soul to God. None can come, 'till effectually Called:

and

If any Man HAVE EARS *to hear, let him hear.* Mark vii. 16.

With Men, it is IMPOSSIBLE : *but not with God.* Ib. x. 27.

Except the Lord had shorten'd those Days, no Flesh should be saved. But, for the ELECTS' *sake, whom*

and they, who are Called effectually, cannot but come. For, as the profound and judicious Mr. Charnock unanswerably argues, " If there be a Counsel [i. e. a Display of " Godlike Wisdom and Design] in framing the lowest Crea-" ture, and in the minutest Passages of Providence; there " must needs be an higher Wisdom in the Government of " Creatures to a supernatural End, and in framing the Soul " to be a Monument of His Glory." *Charnock* on the Attributes, P. 373. — I have met with many Treatises on the Divine Perfections: but with none, which any way equals That of Mr. Charnock. Perspicuity, and Depth; metaphysical Sublimity, and evangelical Simplicity; immense Learning, and plain, but irrefragable, Reasoning; conspire to render that Performance one of the most inæstimable Productions, that ever did Honor to the sanctify'd Judgement and Genius of an Human Being. If I thought myself at all adæquate to the Task, I would endeavor to circulate the Outlines of so rich a Treasure into more Hands, by reducing the Substance of it within the Compass of an *Octavo* Volume. Was such a Design properly executed, a more important Service could hardly be rendered to the Cause of Religion, Virtue, and Knowledge. Many People are frightened at a Folio of more than 800 Pages, who might have both Leisure and Inclination to avail themselves of a well-digested Compendium.

whom He hath chosen, He hath shortened the Days.
―――― *False Prophets should seduce,* IF *it were* POSSIBLE, *even the Elect.* Mark xiii. 20, 22.

One of you, that eateth with me, SHALL *betray me.* Ib. xiv. 18.

All Ye SHALL *be offended, because of Me, this Night.* Ver. 27.

The Hour is COME : *the Son of Man is betrayed,* &c. Ver. 41.

But the Scriptures MUST *be fulfilled.* Ver. 49.

Many Widows were in Israel, but to NONE *of them was Elias sent, save unto Sarepta, a City of Sidon, to a Woman that was a Widow. And many Lepers were in Israel, in the Time of Eliseus the Prophet: but* NONE *of them was cleansed, save Naaman the Syrian.* Luke iv. 26, 27.

I MUST *preach the Kingdom of God to other Citys also: for therefore am I sent.* Ver. 43.

Not one of them [i. e. not a single * *Sparrow*] *is forgotten before God.* Ib. xii. 6.

All Things that are written by the Prophets, concerning the Son of Man, SHALL *be accomplished.*

* " *Oh Blindness to the future,* wisely giv'n,
 " *That each may fill the Circle mark'd by Heav'n!*
 " *Who sees, with equal Eye, as God of All,*
 " *An Hero perish, or a Sparrow fall.*"

POPE.

For He SHALL *be delivered to the Gentiles, and shall be mocked,* &c. Luke xviii. 31.

There shall not an HAIR *of your Head perish.* Ib. xxi. 18. — i. e. before the appointed Time.

Truly, the Son of Man goeth [to Crucifixion and Death] *as it was* DETERMINED: *but Woe unto that Man, by whom He is betrayed.* Ib. xxii. 22. — What a different View did Christ entertain of *Prædestination* and *Necessity*, from that which the Arminians profess to have! The Son of God *connects* two Ideas, which those Gentlemen are for setting at an infinite *Distance:* namely, the DETERMINING DECREE of His Father, by which Moral Evil is effectually permitted; and the PENAL WOE, justly due to the Persons, who, in Consequence of that effectual Permission, are, necessarily, Evil Agents. I shall just touch again upon this Particular, when we come to *John* xix. 11.

This, that is written, MUST *yet be* ACCOMPLISHED *in Me, and He was reckon'd among the Transgressors: for the Things concerning Me have an End* [i.e. they shall every one come to pass]. Luke xxii. 37.

This is YOUR HOUR, *and the Power of Darkness.* Ver. 53.

OUGHT *not Christ to have suffer'd these Things?* Ib. xxiv. 26. — i. e. Was there not a *Necessity* for those very Sufferings, and were they not *inevitable?*

evitable? Certainty itself is not more certain. The entire chain of His Humiliation proceded *just as it should,* without one Circumstance deficient, or one redundant. It all fell out, præcisely, as it *ought*: and ought to have fallen out, præcisely, as it *did.* Why? Because God had *decreed* it, and because Man's Salvation (which was no less decreed) required it. It was prædestinated, that Christ should be deliver'd up to Death, even to the Death of the Cross, and there make His Soul an offering for Sin. But he could not have been betrayed, without a Betrayer: nor crucifyed, without Crucifyers. The *Means,* therefore, no less than the *End,* were necessarily included (as they always are) within the Circle of Divine Præappointment.

But I go on.

That, which is born of the Flesh, is Flesh: and that, which is born of the Spirit, is Spirit. John iii. 6. — What is this but saying? Man, in his natural State, is *necessarily* corrupt: Man, in a regenerate State, is *necessarily* byass'd to God.

If thou knewest the Gift of God, and who it is that saith to thee, Give me to drink; thou wouldst have asked of him. Ib. iv. 11. — But she did *not* know Him, and therefore *could not* so pray to Him. Our Lord, however, knew *her* to be one of his Elect, and that the Time of her Conversion was very near. And, that she might be converted præcisely at the very Time appointed, *He* MUST NEEDS *go through* the Territory of *Samaria.* John iv. 4.

The Hour is coming, and now is, when the Dead [elect Souls, but hitherto unregenerated, and of Course dead to God] SHALL *hear the* [converting] *Voice of the Son of God; and, hearing, they* SHALL *live.* Ib. v. 25.— All true Conversion is wrought by *invincible* Power. The Dead *necessarily* continue so, 'till they are *necessarily* raised to life. A dead Soul, no more than a dead Body, can neither *quicken* itself, nor *hinder* God from doing it. Whoever goes to Christ and Heaven, goes thither by gracious *Necessity :* a Necessity so powerfull, that it even makes him *willing* to go.

All that the Father giveth me, SHALL *come to me.* Chap. vi. 37. — They come *necessarily :* i. e. they cannot but believe with the Faith which is of the Operation of God.

This is the Father's Will, who sent me, that, of ALL *which he hath given me, I should lose* NOTHING; *but should raise it up again at the last Day.* Ver. 39. — God's Will is Necessity itself.

No Man CAN *come to Me, except the Father, who hath sent Me, draw him.* ——— *It is written in the Prophets, And they* [i. e. my People] *shall be all taught of God.* Every Man, therefore, that

hath

hath heard and hath learned [i. e. who has been drawn] *of the Father,* COMETH *unto Me.* John vi. 44, 45.— Neceſſity, on both ſides! *'Till* drawn, none can come: and, *when* drawn, none can ſtay away.

Therefore ſaid I unto you, that no Man CAN *come unto Me, except it be* GIVEN *to him of my Father.* Ver. 65.

They ſought to take Him: but no Man laid Hands on Him, BECAUSE *His Hour was not yet come.* Chap. vii. 30.—'Till then, their Hands were tyed and bound with the inviſible, but adamantin, Chain of Neceſſity. And yet, I ſuppoſe, becauſe they did not *ſee* nor *feel* the Chain, they looked upon themſelves as *Self-determining* Free-Agents!

Whoſoever committeth Sin, is the Servant [δȣλ☉, the Slave] *of Sin.* Chap. viii. 34. — But, according to the Arminian View of Things, it is *ſuch* a Slavery as was never heard of before: the *Slave* is at *perfect Liberty* all the while! I cannot believe this. On the contrary, I believe what follows:

If the Son ſhall MAKE *you free, ye* SHALL *be free indeed.* Ver. 36. — Obſerve, 'till Chriſt *make* us free from the Guilt and Dominion of Sin, we are, *neceſſarily,* in Thraldom to both. If He deliver us, we are, *neceſſarily,* emancipated from each.

Why do ye not underſtand my ſpeech? even becauſe ye CANNOT *hear my Word.* John viii. 43.—A plain, pertinent, deciſive Reaſon.

He that is of God, heareth God's Words: ye therefore hear them not, BECAUSE *ye are not of God.* Ver. 47.—Either not choſen; or, at leaſt, not yet drawn and taught; of Him.

I MUST *work the Works of Him that ſent Me, while it is Day.* Chap. ix. 4. Chriſt was under a *Neceſſity* of doing ſo. He *could not* do any other.

Jeſus ſaid, For Judgement I am come into this World: that they, who ſee not, might ſee; and that they, who ſee, may be made blind. Ver. 39.—Can any Thing be more ſtrongly expreſſed than This?

A Stranger will they not follow, but will flee from him: for they know not the Voice of Strangers. Chap. x. 5.—i. e. The converted Elect diſapprove of falſe Teachers, as *neceſſarily* as Sheep run away from a ſtrange Man they are afraid of.

Other Sheep I have, which are not of this Fold: them alſo I MUST *bring, and they* SHALL *hear my Voice.* Ver. 16.—I *muſt*: and they *ſhall.* What is this but double Neceſſity?

Ye believe not, BECAUSE *Ye are not of my Sheep, as I ſaid unto you.* Ver. 26.——Conſequently, Faith

Faith hangs, not upon Man's Self-determination, but on God's own Self-determined Election.

I give unto my Sheep eternal Life, and they shall never perish. John x. 28. — i. e. Their Salvation is *necessary*, and cannot be hinder'd.

Lazarus, come forth! Chap. xi. 43. — Was it in Lazarus's Power, *not* to awake and rise up?

Though he had done so many Miracles before them, yet they believed not on Him; THAT *the saying of Esaias the Prophet* MIGHT BE FULLFILLED, *which he spake: Lord, who hath believed our Report? and to whom hath the Arm of the Lord been revealed? Therefore they* COULD NOT *believe,* BECAUSE *Esaias said again,* HE *hath blinded their Eyes, and harden'd their Heart; that they should* NOT *see with their Eyes,* NOR *understand with their Heart, and be converted, and I should heal them.* Chap. xi. 37—40. If an Arminian can extract Free-will and Self-determination from these Flowers; he possesses a very different Alembic, from any which *I* am Master of.

One of you SHALL *betray me:* — — *he it is, to whom I shall* GIVE *a Sop when I have dipped it. And, when He had dipped the Sop, He* GAVE *it to Judas Iscariot, the Son of Simon. And,* AFTER *the Sop, Satan enter'd into him.* THEN *said Jesus unto him, That thou dost, do quickly.* Chap. xiii. 21, 26, 27. — Awefull Process!

I will pray the Father, and He shall give you another Comforter, —— whom the World CANNOT *receive, becaufe it feeth Him not, neither knoweth Him.* John xiv. 16, 17.

Becaufe I live, Ye SHALL *live alfo.* Ver. 19.— Chrift lives and reigns in Glory, *neceffarily:* and fo muft His People.

Ye have not chofen Me, but I have chofen You, and ordained You; that ye fhould go and bring forth Fruit, and that your Fruit fhould remain. Chap. xv. 16.

They have both feen and hated both Me and my Father: but this cometh to pafs, THAT *the Word might be* FULLFILLED *which is written in their law; They hated Me without a Caufe.* Ver. 24, 25.

Father, THE HOUR *is come.* Chap. xvii. 1. — The prædeftined Seafon of my Crucifixion and Death.

None of them [none of my Apoftles] *is loft, but the Son of Perdition, that the Scripture might be fullfilled.* Ver. 12.

The Cup which my FATHER *hath given Me, fhall I not drink it?* Chap. xviii. 11.— A Cup, all whofe Ingredients were mixed in the Father's Decree, and adminifter'd by Providence, tho' Wicked Men were the Inftruments of accomplifhing God's Counfel. *Qui vult Finem, vult etiam Media ad Finem.*

Pilate

Pilate said unto them, Take ye Him, and judge Him according to your Law. The Jews therefore said unto him, It is not lawfull for us to put any Man to Death. That the Saying of Jesus might be FULLFILLED, *which He spake, signifying, by* WHAT *Death he should dye.* John xviii. 31, 32. — God had decreed, and Christ Himself had foretold, that He should dye by *Crucifixion.* But had the Jews accepted of Pilate's Overture, Christ could not have been crucify'd, for that was no Jewish Punishment: He must have been *stoned.* To fullfill both Decree and Prophecy, they were divinely over-ruled, to let the *Romans* be His Executioners: in Consequence of which, He was affixed to the Cross. — NECESSITATION throughout!

Pontius Pilate was a Free-will man. He did not believe *Necessity.* He was a sturdy (not *Self-determiner,* for no Man can be really and truly that; but a) *Self-determinationist:* i. e. he *thought* himself a Self-determining Agent. Hence his Speech to Christ: *Speakest thou not to* ME? *Knowest thou not, that I have Power to crucify thee, and have Power to release thee?* To which the Lamb of God reply'd, *Thou couldst have* NO *Power* AT ALL *against Me, except it were* GIVEN *thee from above: therefore, he, that delivered Me unto thee, hath the greater Sin.* John xix. 10. —

Here,

Here, I presume, Mr. Wesley will step in with his favorite Universal Demonstration, "Not so."—' If the Power both of the Betrayer and of the Crucifyer was *given* them, and *from above* too, i. e. from God Himself; Judas and Pilate could have *no sin at all* in acting as they did, so far from having the *greater* Sin by that Means'. The Methodist must excuse me, if I believe the Testimony of CHRIST, in Preference to any Cavil that can originate in Moor-fields.

Again. I assert, that the Roman Soldiers *had it not in their Power* to break the Messiah's Legs. For that Scripture was *necessarily* to be fullfilled, which had said, *A Bone of Him shall not be broken.* Chap. xix. 33, 36.

On the other hand, I assert, that the Soldier, who penetrated the Messiah's Side, did it *necessarily*. Because, another Scripture had said, *They shall look on Him whom they pierced*; Ver. 37. So sure is that Axiom, *Nihil est in Effectu, quod non fuit in Causâ.*

It was my Intention, to have produced, at much greater Length than I have done in the Close of the foregoing Chapter, the Suffrages of the *Apostles*, also, on behalf of this Doctrine: who offer their Evidence, from every Part of the inspired Epistles. But, at present, I waive this Advantage: and, for Brevity's sake, refer the Reader,

Reader, indiscriminately, to any Portion whatever of those Writings, which he may first open, or on which he may first cast his Eye. Dip where you will, your own *Reason* (abstracted from all Consideration of *Grace*) must instantly perceive, that the illuminated Penmen were as radicated *Necessitarians*, as their Divine Master.

And now, What can a fair and capable Examinant think, of the Arminian *Self-determination* Doctrine? A Doctrine which would impiously graft such a Monster as *Contingency*, on the Religion of JESUS CHRIST ―― a Religion, which, from it's Alpha to it's Omega, presents us with one, grand, unbroken, and indissoluble, System of *Necessity*!

Is it any Wonder, that Men, who consider the Incarnation, Miracles, Prophecys, Perseverance, Sufferings, Death, and Salvation, of the MESSIAH Himself, as Things of *Chance*; should likewise maintain *all other* Events to be equally *fortuitous*?

Hence, the Alertness and Rapidity, with which many of our modern Arminians (more *consistent*, but at the same Time more *atheistical*, than the Generality of their Prædecessors), not content with trampling on God's *Decrees*, are now verging toward a flat *Denial* even of God's *absolute* and *unlimited Knowledge*. Justly sensible, that

their

their whole fairy Scheme of Chance, Uncertainty, and Contingency, is quite untenable, on the Position of Infallible-Præscience; they make no Scruple to rob (if they were able) the Deity Himself of a Perfection essential to His very Being, rather than not stick the Feather of Freewill in the Cap of Man!

CHAPTER VI.

An Argument for NECESSITY, *deduced from the Balance of Human* LIFE *and* DEATH.

WAS it not for that universal *Necessitation*, which results from the effective and permissive Will of God; all Things would be, in a Moment, unhinged, disjointed, and reversed. Endless Confusion, wild Irregularity, and the most horrible Disorder (to which the *Materia prima*, or Chaos, was Harmony itself), would prevail throughout the Natural and the Moral World.

The Property of *Attraction*, by which the Earth, and every other Mass of Matter, cohære respectively into one Body, and become capable of of the moſt rapid Motion, without Diſſipation of their conſtituent Particles; is one happy Effect of PHYSICAL Neceſſity. Analogous to which, but of incomparably greater Importance, is that *ineluctabilis Ordo Rerum*, or unalterable Contexture of Antecedents and Conſequents, wiſely præ-eſtabliſhed in the Uncreated Mind: through the concealed energy of whoſe unerring Appointment, every finite intelligent Being both *is* and *does*, præciſely, neither more nor leſs, than the ſaid unerring Wiſdom of the Creator *deſigned*, or reſolved to *permit*. And this is what I ſhould chuſe to call MORAL Neceſſity.

Suppoſing that Calculation to be juſt, which æſtimates the adult Inhabitants of our own Globe at about One Hundred and Fifty Millions; or let their real Amount be what it may; who can poſſibly conceive the boundleſs Diſtractions and Deſolations, which muſt every where enſue, were ſo great a Number of *fallen* Beings (like ramping Horſes turned looſe into a Field) endued with a Liberty of *Self-determination*, and left at large to the *Exerciſe* of it! For we muſt take the *Exerciſe*, and the outward *Operations* conſequent upon it, into the Account: elſe mere *Self-determination* would anſwer no other End, than that of tantalizing and tormenting it's reſpective Poſſeſſors.—'Tis well for us, that, notwithſtanding

our

our wild and licentious Arrogations of Sovereignty, the same Almighty Parent, who, without asking our Consent, whirls our Planet and our Persons round the Sun; does, with equal Certainty, and with as little Ceremony, roll us, and the Inhabitants of all the Worlds He has created, on the central Axis of his own Decree.

We have been gravely told, that this Representation of Things is *Heathenism*. You should rather call it, *Bible-ism*. For, THAT *Fate*, or *Necessity*, which the antient Vulgar thought proper to worship as a goddess; was, in their Idea, the Daughter of a blind, fickle Princess, called, *Fortune*, or *Chance*: who was, herself, the fabled Daughter of a no less fickle old Gentleman, named *Oceanus*. To which blind Lady, and her unsteady Father, the Scheme of CHRISTIAN Necessity is not in the least related, either by Consanguinity, or Alliance.

I must, however, acquit the Wiser of the Heathens, from the Absurdity of looking upon *Chance*, or *Fortune*, as a Reality. Sensible Men knew better, and laughed at the unphilosophical Chimæra. Nor is the Antiquity, of the Word itself, extremely high. 'Tis acknowledged, on all Hands, that Τυχη (from whence the Romans took their *Fortuna*) was a Term, invented long after the Times of *Hesiod* and of *Homer* (in whose

Writings

Writings it no where occurs); and was spawned by the atheistical Imagination of subsequent Poets: from whom (I think) *Ancus Martius* adopted it, and, by building a Temple to it's Honor, introduced it, as a Deity, among the Romans.

It ill becomes the *Arminians* to talk of *Heathenism*. Let 'em draw a solid Line, if they can, between *Fortune*, and *Contingency*. Let 'em shew us, how the Result of *Self-determination* differs from *Chance*. Let 'em reconcile their imaginary αὐτεξούσιον, with the necessary *Dependency* of created Beings, and with the never-ceasing *Agency* of an * universally particular *Providence*. When they have wrought these, and a few other similar Impossibilitys; I will THEN absolve their Scheme

---

* Mr. Pope asks:

When the loose Mountain trembles from on high,
Shall Gravitation cease, 'cause You go by?

I answer, *Yes*. Either Gravitation *shall cease*, while I go by; or I shall, in some way or other, be secured from suffering by it's Effect; unless the Will of God, to which all second Causes are absolutely subordinate, commission the " loose Mountain" to do me an Injury. I am of the great Mr. Charnock's Mind, that " There is Understanding, in " every Motion: and an Eye, in the very Wheel that goes " over us and crushes us." (Charnock on the Attributes, P. 419.)

from

from *Heathenism*. I will even acquit it of *Atheism*.

Birth and *Death* are the æra and the Period, whose Interval constitutes the Thread of Man's visible Existence on Earth. Let us examine, whether those important *Extremes* be, or be not, unalterably fixed by the necessitating Providence of God. If it appear, that they *are*; we may the more easily believe, that all the *intercurrent* Events are under the Controll and Direction of the same infallible Hand.

I have heard it affirmed, that Descartes, the French Philosopher, was so consistent a Free-willer, as to have believed, that *Death* itself is absolutely subject to Human *Self-Determination*: that he consequently imagined, he had it in his Power to protract his own Age to any Extent he pleased, or to cut it præcisely as short as he himself chose: and would, very liberally, call any of his departed Friends, who had dyed with Reluctance, Fools; for *consenting* to a Change they did not wish to experience. The antient Romans, notwithstanding the Adulterations, with which the Doctrine of *Free-will* (and it's natural Attendent, *Scepticism*) debased and corrupted their Theology; were yet, in general, so decent, as to acknowledge, that *Death* lay at the Disposal of a Deity, less capricious than Fortune, and

and more powerfull than any created Will. Hence, their occafional Reciprocation of MORS and FATUM. To intimate, that Men cannot *dye*, 'till God *pronounce* their Doom: and that, when He *fatus eft*, or *iffues the Word* of Summons, the earthly Vehicle can detain it's Gueft no longer. —— Poor Defcartes, with all his Dreams of Free-will, found himfelf obliged to dye, at the Age of Fifty-four!

I take the *Ratio formalis*, or præcife Nature, of Death; to be neither more nor lefs than the Effect of SEPARATION. The *Separation of Spirit from Matter* is the immediate Caufe, and feems to exhauft the Idea, of Animal Death. Now, only the fame Power, which at firft *joined*, can afterwards *fever*, the two Principles. Let the permitted *Means* of diffolving the Union be what they may, the *Diffolution itfelf* is an Act of God.

Whoever confiders the relative Alterations, the domeftic Revolutions, the Circulation of Property, and a Multitude of other negative and pofitive Confequences, which, either directly or remotely, follow on the Deceafe of the meaneft Human Individual; muft foon perceive, that, was not the Sceptre of Death fwayed by the De- terminations of Infinite Wifdom, fuch *partial* Inconveniences muft enfue, as would, in their complicated Amount, materially affect, if not

entirely

entirely reverse, the *whole* System of sublunary Events. Some People (for Instance) would live *too long.* Others would dye *too soon.* Some would leave their assigned Work *unfinished:* from whence the Deity would be disappointed of His views, and surprized with a Chasm in His Administration of Government. Others would survive to *do more* than their allotted Business. From whence, the Divine Plan, would be disconcerted; the well-compacted Web become loose, broken, and entangled; and the Administration of Providence degenerate into a Jumble of Confusion, Perplexity, and absolute Anarchy. In one word: God could not say, to any one of His Creatures, what he really does say to all and each of them; *Hitherto* SHALT *thou come, and* NO FARTHER.

Our *Entrance* into Life is determined, and adjusted, by the same disposing Hand, which fixes and regulates our Departure. *Necessity* brings us into the World: and *Necessity* carrys us out of it. What Man upon earth could help his being born at the very Time and Place he was? or could hinder himself from being the Son of such and such Parents? or alter a Thousand concurring Circumstances, by which his subsequent State, and his very Cast of Mind, were effectually and necessarily stamped? How absurd, then, must

it

it be, to imagine that the Line, tho' *spun* at first by the Hand of Necessity; is afterwards *conducted*, and at last *cut off*, by the no-Fingers of Contingency! For it is impossible to conceive any Thing so absolutely contingent and uncertain, as the Operations, and the Exit, of a Self-determining Actor. Especially, if we suppose him (and the Arminian Scheme *does* so suppose him) to live in a World, where all about him is as precarious as himself; and where the great Sheet of Events, instead of being let down by the four Corners from Heaven, is only a fortuitous Complication of flimsy Threads, much of which is still liable to Unravelment, and the whole of which might never have been woven at all.

Might *Charles* the First have been the Son of Cromwell's Parents? And might *Cromwell* have been born legal Heir to the English Crown? Was it possible for Sir *Robert Walpole* to have been Prime Minister to Queen *Elizabeth*; and for Sir *Francis Walsingham* to have been Secretary of State to King *George* the Second? Yet, all these Impossibilitys, and Millions of others, *might* have happen'd, upon the Arminian Scheme of *Chance*. A Scheme, which, if admitted, turns every Thing upside down, and knocks ev'ry Thing out of Joint:

Diruit,

Diruit, ædificat, mutat quadrata rotundis.

Why was Friar *Bacon*, and not Sir *Isaac Newton*, born in the thirteenth Century? Why were not the living Ornaments, of the present Generation, born an Hundred, or five Hundred, Years back? or reserved to Ages as remotely future? Arminianism may tell me, that " All this is " *casual:* and that it was a CHANCE, not only " *when* and *where* the present Race of Men " might be born, and *what Departments* they " should fill; *how* they should act, and *how* " and *when* they shall dye; but whether they " should so much as *exist* at first." I, on the contrary, discern such incontestable Traces of Wisdom, Propriety, and Design, in the Distribution of particular Men through successive Periods of Time, and in the whole Connection of Event with Event; that, for my own Part, I *necessarily* conclude, so regular a Chain could not possibly be hammer'd in the Cyclopæan Den of Contingency: but that every depending Link is fitted and fixed into each other, by the SUPREME INTELLIGENCE Himself; the Disposals of whose Providence, like the Covenant of His Grace, are *order'd in all Things, and sure* *.

As

---

* 2 Sam. xxiii. 5. — Those of us, who go to Church, profess ourselves to be " *Tyed* and *bound* with the *Chain* of
" our

As lightly as some People think of the *Bible*, that Book is the Fountain of true *Metaphysics*. A Book, no less weighty, with the Treasures of *philosophic* Wisdom; than bright, with the healing Beams of evangelical Consolation. To this blessed Oracle, I now refer the Quæstion; *Whether Human* Birth *and* Death *be not the Effects of* Divine Necessitation?

I shall not be very prolix. Two or three plain and pertinent Testimonys will answer the same Purpose, as two or three Hundred. — Let us begin with the Article of *Birth*.

Rachel said unto Jacob, Give me Children, or else I dye. And Jacob's Anger was kindled against Rachel: and he said, Am I in God's *stead?* Gen. xxx. 1, 2.

Joseph said unto his Father, They are my Sons, whom God *hath given me in this Place.* Gen. xlviii. 9.

Thy Hands *have made me, and fashioned me together, round about.* Job x. 8.

Thou art He that took me out of the Womb. Psal. xxii. 9.

Who holdeth [better render'd, *Who* putteth] *our Soul in Life, and suffereth not our Feet to be*

" our *Sins*." Why, then, should we deem ourselves too Grand to be *tyed* and *bound*, with the *good*, tho' not always *perceivable*, Chain of Providential Necessity?

moved. Pſalm lxvi. 9.—i. e. God *gave* us Life at firſt; and *keeps* us alive, 'till it is His Pleaſure to untye the Knot that binds us to the Body.

Lo, Children are an Heritage of the Lord. Pſalm cxxvii. 3.—Or, as the Liturgy Tranſlation reads, *Lo, Children and the Fruit of the Womb are an Heritage and Gift that cometh of the Lord.*

And the Caſe ſpeaks for itſelf. The Birth of every ſingle Infant is productive of no leſs than *everlaſting* Conſequences. Every Infant (even ſuppoſing him to dye ſuch) is an *immortal* Being. But, ſuppoſing he lives to bear an active Part in Life, Society is very materially concerned in his Behavior. Each adult Individual makes important Movements, in the grand Circular Scale of Events. The Alteration of a ſingle Birth, or of a ſingle Death, from the firſt Period of Time 'till now, would have occaſion'd ſuch a *Difference*, that neither the Viſible, nor the Inviſible World, would have been *as it is:* i. e. ſomething would have been wrong, either in Defect, or in Redundancy. None of us can tell, what may hang on the Nativity of the meaneſt Infant that is born of Woman. But the Creator knows: for He is acquainted with His own Decrees, and orders Matters accordingly.

Thou haſt covered me [i. e. cloathed my Soul with a material Body] *in my Mother's Womb:*—
———*In*

―― *In thy Book* [of Decree and Providence] *all my Members were written.* Pſalm cxxxix. 13, 16.

To every Thing there is a Seaſon, and a Time to every Purpoſe under the Heaven; [i. e. God has fixed an exact Point of Time, for the Accompliſhment of all His Decrees: among which fixed and exact Points of Time, are] *a Time to be* BORN, *and a Time to dye.* Eccleſ. iii. 1, 2.

Who * *formeth the Spirit of Man within him.* Zech. xii. 1.

* This Text, and many others of ſimilar Import, ſeem to intimate, that the *Body* is *firſt* made; and that the *Soul*, commanded into Exiſtence for the Purpoſe, is united to the Body thus previouſly provided for it's Reception. The direct Source, however, of the Soul, is an Enquiry attended with great metaphyſical Difficultys; whether we ſuppoſe it to be of God's immediate Creation, or to originate from parental Tranſmiſſion. Much may be ſaid for each Hypotheſis: and ſeveral weighty Objections lye againſt both. It becomes us, probably, to confeſs, that Scripture has not clearly decided the Point: and, of Courſe, that we know very little of the Matter. *In talibus Quæſtionibus*, as WITSIUS ſays on another myſterious Occaſion, *magis mihi placet hæſitantis Ingenii Modeſtia, quàm inconſiderata determinandi Pervicacia* (Diſſert. de Michaele). 'This only we are ſure of, that God Himſelf, and not Chance, is (either mediately, or immediately, according to the good Pleaſure of His own Will) the Formator, and the Governor, of every Spirit, and of every Body, in the Univerſe.

God, who separated me from my Mother's Womb. Gal. i. 15.

Does it not appear, even from these few Passages, that the Doctrine of *fortuitous Nativity* is as false and ridiculous, as that of *æquivocal Generation?*

And the Doctrine of *fortuitous Death* is like unto it. Witness the following Evidence.

The Time drew near that Israel MUST *dye.* Gen. xlvii. 29. —— Observe, 1. A Time for Jacob's Death was præfixed of God: and 'tis therefore called, THE *Time*; meaning, that præcise Time, and no other. 2. The Time *drew near:* and the holy Man was like a Racer in View of the Goal, or like a Mariner in Sight of the Haven where he would be. 3. He *must* dye; which Expression does not denote any Unwillingness in Jacob; but the *Certainty* of his Departure, when the destined Moment should arrive.

Can any Incident be more seemingly fortuitous, than what we commonly call *Homicide,* or one Man's *Undesignedly killing* of another? And yet this, when it comes to pass, is according to the secret Will of God: who is positively affirmed to *deliver* the slain Party *into the Hand* of the Slayer. Exod. xxi. 31.

He [i. e. God] *is thy Life, and the Length of thy Days.* Deut. xxx. 20. —— The *Author* of That, and the *Measurer* of These.

The LORD *killeth, and maketh alive:* HE *bringeth down to the Grave, and bringeth up.* 1 Sam. ii. 6. — Which exactly comports with what God says of Himself: *I, even I, am He; and there is no God with Me. I kill, and I make alive: I wound, and I heal: neither is there Any that can deliver out of My Hand.* Deut. xxxii. 39.

Is there not an APPOINTED *Time to Man upon Earth? Are not his Days also like the Days of an Hireling?* Job. vii. 1. — The stipulated Hours, of an Hireling's Labor, are ascertained beforehand: they consist of so many, and no more.

Thou hast granted me Life and Favor; and thy Visitation hath preserved my Spirit. Job. x. 12.

In whose Hand is the Soul of every living Thing, and the Breath of all Mankind. Job. xii. 10.

Man's *Days are* DETERMINED; *the Number of his Months is with Thee: Thou hast appointed his Bounds, which he cannot pass.* ——— *All the Days of my* APPOINTED TIME *will I wait, 'till my Change come.* Job xiv. 5, 14.

Thou prevailest for ever against him [i. e. Man cannot possibly extend his own Life a single Moment beyond thy Decree]: *Thou changest his Countenance* [by Death], *and sendest him away.* Job xiv. 20. — Sendest his *Body* to the Grave, and his *Soul* to another World.

Lord, make me to know my End, and the Measure of my Days; what it is. Psalm xxxix. 4. — But, unless God had *fixed* David's END, and had *determined* the MEASURE of his Days; the Psalmist would here have asked a Quæstion, to which God Himself could only have answered, " O Son of " Jesse, I know no more of the Matter, than " You do. You have started a Problem, which " I am unable to resolve: for there is no *measuring* in the Case."

THOU *turnest Man to Destruction.* Psalm xc. 3.

There is no Man that hath Power over the Spirit, to retain the Spirit [i. e. to retain the Soul in the Body, beyond the Term divinely præfixed]; *neither hath he Power in the Day of Death.* Eccles. viii. 8.

Behold, I will add unto thy Days fifteen Years. Isai. xxxviii. 5. — Hezekiah thought, that his Lease was just expiring, and that his Soul must, almost immediately, turn out of it's earthly Cottage. *No,* says God; You have fifteen Years to be added to those of your Days which are elapsed: and the said future Years are of *my* adding, no less than were the Years that are past. " Oh, but God said to Hezekiah, *I have heard* " *thy Prayer, and have seen thy Tears.*" True. And what does this prove? Not that God's Decree

cree is a * Weathercock, shifting, and changing, and veering about, just as the Breath of Man's Freewill happens to blow: BUT, that the Scriptural Axiom is right, which says, *Lord, thou hast heard the Desire of the Afflicted:* THOU PREPAREST *their Heart* [to pray for such Things as Thou hast decreed to give], *and thine Ear hearkeneth thereto.* — I must farther observe: that, if there be any Meaning in Words, Hezekiah, *could not* dye, 'till the remaining fifteen Years had run out; and *could not but* dye, when they were.

Which of you, by taking Thought, can add one Cubit, πρὸς ἡλικιαν αὐτε, *to his Term of Life?* Matt. vi. 27. Let us hear the Reflections of that learned, pious, and truly respectable Arminian, Dr. *Hammond,* on this Text. After observing,

---

* "Prayer moves God, and overcomes Him, not by causing any *Change* in the Divine Will: for God is immutable; and what Good He does in Time for his People, He purposed before any Time was. But Prayer is said to overcome Him, because He *then* gives, what, from Eternity, He purposed to give, upon their praying to Him. For, when God decreed what He would *do* for his Saints, He also purposed that they should *pray* for the same: Ezek. xxxvi. 37. —— Prayer's Midwifry shall be used, to deliver the Mercys which God purposeth and promiseth. —— God's *Purpose* to give, doth not discharge us from our *Duty* to ask." GURNALL's Christian Armor, Vol. IV. P. 17.

that

that ἡλικία sometimes denotes " The *Quantity*,
or *Stature*, of the Body"; he adds : " So also
" doth it ordinarily signify, *Age* (and so doth
" קומתא, which the *Syriac* here uses); and may
" possibly do so here : 1. Because the Dehorta-
" tion, which this [Question of Christ's] is
" brought to enforce, was particularly That con-
" cerning Solicitude for the *Life:* and to That,
" this will be very proper, of *our not being able*
" *to* ADD, *by all our Solicitude, the* LEAST *Pro-*
" *portion to our Age,* to enlarge the *Period of Life*
" πηχυν ἕνα, *one Cubit,* i. e. one *smallest* Measure
" or Proportion, *beyond what God hath* SET *us.*
" — 2. It will be observable, that *one Cubit* be-
" ing here set down as a *very small* Measure;
" would yet be a *very great* Proportion, being
" apply'd to the *Stature* of the Body. Nay,
" such as are come to their full Growth (as the
" far greatest Part of Christ's Auditors were)
" *could not* thus hope to add *one thousandth Part*
" *of a Cubit* to their *Stature.* — On the other
" Side, a *Cubit* will seem but a *small* Part, to
" the many Years of a long Life. And he that
" is of the *fullest Growth,* may yet hope to *enlarge*
" the Period of his *Life:* and to That, gene-
" rally, Men's Solicitude is apply'd; by Diet,
" Physic, &c. to acquire *long Life,* not to in-
" crease their *Stature.*—3. The Word πηχυς, *Cubit,*
" is

" is ordinarily a Measure of the *Longitude* of any
" *Space:* and, particularly, of a *Race*; to which
" Man's *Life* is compared. Job ix. 25. 2 Tim.
" iv. 7."

This Truth may be farther argued, from another Passage, cited also in a præceding Chapter: viz. *Matt.* x. 29, 30. For, if not a *Sparrow* can dye, without God's express Commission; much less can a *Man.* And, if the very *Hairs* of our Heads are number'd, much more our *Days.*

God *giveth, unto all, Life, and Breath, and all Things: and hath made of one Blood all Nations of Men, for to dwell on all the Face of the Earth; and hath determined the Times, before appointed; and the Bounds of their Habitation. —— —— For in Him we live, and are moved, and have our Being.* Acts xvii. 25, 26, 28.—Observe: 1. God is the *Giver* of Animal Life, as well as of every Thing else. — 2. He has multiply'd us all, from one Stock: viz. Adam. — 3. The *Times,* i. e. the proper Seasons, of our Birth and Death, and of all that we shall do or suffer between the Starting-Post and the Goal, are *determined,* or marked out with Certainty and Exactness, by Him Himself. — 4. This *Determination,* or Adjustment, of our *Times;* is not a modern Act of God, arising *è Re natâ,* or from any present Emergency of Circumstances and Situation

of

of Affairs: but a *Determination,* inconceivably antient. The *Times* were FORE-*appointed*; even from everlasting: for no *new* Determination can take Place in God, without a *Change,* i. e. without the *Destruction,* of His Essence. *Quævis Mutatio Mors est.* — 5. The very *Places,* which People inhabit, are here positively averr'd to be *determined* and *fore-appointed* of God. And 'tis very right it should be so. Else, some Places might be over-stocked with Inhabitants, and others totally deserted: which would necessarily draw after it the most pernicious Consequences; as Stagnation of Agriculture, Famine, Pestilence, and general Ruin to the Human Species. Whereas, by Virtue of God's having *fore-appointed* and *determined* the *Bounds of our Habitations*; we are properly *sifted* over the Face of the Earth, so as to answer all the social and higher Purposes of providential Wisdom. — 6. If DEITY has condescended to *determine,* in what particular *Places* our Bodys shall dwell; why should it appear strange, that He should also determine *how long* our *Souls* shall dwell in their *Bodys?* Adverbs of Time are no less important, than Adverbs of Place. Nor, indeed, could Omnipotence itself determine the *ibi,* without likewise determining the *quando,* and the *diu.* — Especially, when we

consider,

consider, 7. That *in* HIM *we*, every Moment, *live, and are moved, and do exist.*

Moreover, if Christ's own Testimony will have any Weight with Self-determinationists, the following Text, exclusively of all others, will set the Point above Dispute: where our Lord roundly affirms, that He Himself keeps *the Keys of Hell and of Death.* Rev. i. 18. Which Declaration holds true, in *every* Sense the Words are capable of. He *openeth, and no Man can shut: and shutteth, and no Man can open.* Rev. iii. 7.

Nor is Divine Providence the Distributor of Death to MAN alone. The very *Beasts* themselves, which are, by many, supposed to *perish* utterly; are immortal, 'till God cut their Thread. *Thou hidest thy Face: they are troubled. Thou takest away their Breath: they die; and return to their Dust.* Psalm civ. 29. — It should be remember'd, that this is more directly spoken, concerning those *small and great Beasts, and creeping Things innumerable,* which inhabit the *Sea.* So that FISHES themselves, from a Whale to a Periwinkle, have the Creator Himself for the Disposer of their Lives, and the Determiner of their Deaths!

From the Evidence alledged, concise and superficial as my Allegations have been; we may fairly (and, I think, unanswerably) conclude: that CONTINGENCY *has nothing to do with* BIRTHS, *or* BURIALS; *and*, confequently, that CHANCE *never yet added, nor ever will add,* * " a fingle Unit to " the Bills of Mortality."

If, therefore, the *initial Point*, from whence we ftart; and the *ultimate Goal*, which terminates our Race; be thus Divinely and Unchangeably *fixed*: is it reafonable to fuppofe, that Chance, or any Freewill but the Freewill of Deity alone, may fabricate the *intermediate* Links of a Chain, whofe two *Extremes* are held immovably faft in the Hands of God Himfelf? — Impoffible.

* For this Phrafe, *a fingle Unit to the Bill of Mortality*, fee Lord Chefterfield's Letters: Lett. 336.

CHAP.

CHAPTER VII.

The ſuppoſed GLOOMINESS *of Neceſſity, conſider'd.* — *The* ORIGIN *of Doctrinal Neceſſity.* — *Conciſe View of* MANICHÆISM. — *The Nature of* EVIL *enquired into.* — *Curious* CONVERSATION-*Pieces of three Modern Philoſophizers.* — *Several* ASSEMBLYS *of* DIVINES *vindicated.* — ARMINIANS *themſelves ultimately forced to make* NECESSITY *their Refuge.* — CONCLUSION *of the preſent Eſſay.*

1. GREAT declamatory Pains have been taken, to ſet the Syſtem of *Neceſſity* in a very "*gloomy*" Point of View: and to miſrepreſent it, as made up of nothing but *Clouds, and Shades, and thick Darkneſs*. The ſame has been ſaid of *Religion* at large, and of *Virtue* itſelf. But are Virtue and Religion *therefore* deformed and black, becauſe their Beauty and Luſtre do not ſtrike a libertine Eye? No more is the Scheme of *Neceſſity* tinged with real Gloom, on Account of a proud or prejudiced Freewiller's being pleaſed to aſſert it.

" I have

[120]

"I have sometimes beheld," says an elegant Writer, "a Ship of War, several Leagues off at Sea. It seemed to be a *dim, cloudy* Something, hovering on the Skirts of the Horizon: contemptibly mean, and not worthy of a Moment's Regard.—But, as the floating Citadel approached, the Masts arose. The Sails swelled out. It's stately Form, and curious Propertys, struck the Sight. It was no longer a *shapeless* Mass, or a *Blot* in the Prospect: but the *Master-piece* of human Contrivance, and the *noblest* Spectacle in the World of Art." *Hervey*'s Theron and Aspasio, Dialogue 5.

Arminianism, if you please, is a Region of Darkness: but Necessity, a Land of * Light.

For

---

* The pretended *Gloominess* of Necessity is urged, with most Appearance (and 'tis but Appearance) of Plausibility, against that Branch of Scripture-Metaphysics, which relates to the Decree of *Reprobation*. Let me, for a Moment, weigh the pretended Horror of this Principle: a Principle, which occurrs so positively and repeatedly, again and again, in almost every Page of the Bible; that the Existence of God does not admit of more strong and explicit Proof, from the inspired Volume, than does the awfull Reality of Non-Election. What I here mean to observe on this Subject, I shall give, in the Words of Part of a Letter, which I lately sent to a very eminent Anti-Calvinian Philosopher. "Why are Calvin's Doctrines represented as *gloomy?* Is it gloomy, to believe, that the *far greater Part* of the Human Race are

made

For I should be glad to be informed, wherein consists the *Chearfullness* of believing, that the greater

made for *end'ess Happiness?* There can, I think, be no reasonable Doubt entertained, concerning the Salvation of very young Persons. If (as some, who have versed themselves in this Kind of Speculation, affirm) about one Half of Mankind dye in *Infancy*;— And if, as indubitable Observation proves, a very considerable Number of the remaining Half dye in early *Childhood*;— And if, as there is the strongest Reason to think, *many Millions* of those, who live to maturer Years, in every successive Generation, have their Names in the Book of LIFE: then, what a very small Portion, comparatively, of the Human Species, falls under the Decree of Præterition and Non-Redemption!

" This View of Things, I am persuaded, will, to an Eye so philosophic as your's, at least open a very chearfull *Vista* through the ' Gloom'; if not entirely turn the imaginary Darkness into Sunshine. For, with respect to the few Reprobate, we *may*, and we *ought* to, resign the Disposal of them, implicitly, to the Will of that only King who can do no wrong: instead of Summoning the Almighty to take his Tryal at the Tribunal of *our* Speculations, and of setting up ourselves as Judges of Deity."

I might have added, That the Purpose of God according to *Election* is not restrained to Men, either of any particular *Country*, or *Age* of Time, or religious *Denomination*. Undoubtedly, there are elect *Jews*, elect *Mahometans*, and elect *Pagans*. In a Word, countless Millions of Persons, whom Christ hath *redeemed unto God, by his Blood, out of* EVERY *Kindred, and Tongue, and People, and Nation.* Rev. v. 9.

greater Part, if not the Whole, of sublunary Events, even those of *endless* Concern not excepted, are deliver'd over to the Management of an imaginary goddess, called *Chance*; the mere Creature of Poetic Fiction, and the most unmeaning Sound that was ever admitted into Language?

" Oh, but we deny *Chance*, and maintain *Free-*
" *will*." Be so good as to shew me, *how* you can maintain self-determining Freewill, without setting up the blind Daughter of Oceanus upon her Pedestal. If the WILL of Man be free, with a Liberty *ad utrumlibet*; and if his ACTIONS be the Offspring of his Will; such of his Actions, which are not yet wrought, must be both radically and eventually *uncertain:* as depending, for their Futurition, on an *uncertain Cause*, viz. on the *uncertain* Volitions of an Agent, who *may*, or may *not*, incline himself to the Performance of those Actions. It is, therefore, a *Chance*, whether they shall ever be performed, or no. For *Chance*, and *Uncertainty*, are only two Words for the same Idea. So that every Assertor of *Self-determination* is, in fact, whether he mean it or no, a

---

Only take a fair and dispassionate Survey of the Matter, as it *is*; and the Arminian Outcrys will be found a *Vox, et præterea nihil*. For, *Who can count the Dust of Jacob, or the Number of the fourth Part of* God's Elect *Israel?*

Worshipper

Worshipper of the Heathen Lady, named, *Fortune*; and an ideal Deposer of PROVIDENCE from it's Throne.

Could Providence be really dethroned, with as much Ease as it's Influence is denied; dreadfull indeed would be the State of Things. For my Part, I think, that all the *Chearfullness* lyes on the Side of *Necessity*. And for this plain Reason: because, that Infinite Wisdom, which made, or permitted, us to BE what we are, and to be CIRCUMSTANCED as we are; knows better, what to do with us, than we could possibly know how to dispose of our own Selves.

'Tis *my* Happiness, to be convinced, that *my Times are in God's Hand*, Psalm xxxi. 15. and that *His Kingdom ruleth over all*. Psalm ciii. 19. If any Others can extract *Comfort* from considering themselves as Vessels sailing over a dangerous Ocean, without *Pilot*, without *Chart*, without *Insurance*, and without *Convoy*, to a Coast unknown; much good may their Comfort do them. I desire none of it.

Gloomy as the Doctrine of Christian Necessity is ignorantly affirmed to be; 'tis the only Principle, upon which any Person can, truly and consistently, adopt that animating Apophthegm, so perpetually in the Mouth of St. Chrysostom, *Blessed be God, for* EVERY *Thing that comes to pass!* —

Whereas, the genuine Language of an afflicted Freewiller is, *Alas! Alas! what an* UNLUCKY ACCIDENT *was this!* The very Exclamation, which might be expected to issue from the Lips of a melancholy, desponding Atheist.

If unreserved *Resignation*, to the wise and fatherly Disposals of God; if *Contentedness* and *Complacency*, within our several Sphæres and Stations; if *Thankfulness*, for the Blessings we enjoy; if the Exercise of *Candor*, *Lenity*, and *Compassion*, toward our mistaken, our offending, and our afflicted fellow-Creatures; if *Humility*, and a deep Sense of our absolute *Dependence* on the Arm of Omnipotent Love, for Preservation or Deliverance from Evil, and for the Continuance or Increase of Good; if the pleasing Conviction that *nothing can hurt us*, except God's own Hand first sign the License; if a just *Confidence*, that He will never sign any such License, but to answer the best and wisest Ends; if an unshaken Persuasion, that whatever He DOES is, and must be, *absolutely*, and *directly*, RIGHT; and that whatever He PERMITS to be done, is, and must be, *relatively, conducively,* and *finally*, RIGHT :— If these lovely Virtues, and felicitating Views (Virtues and Views which no Necessitarian can, consistently, be without), have any Thing *gloomy* in them; it will follow, that the Sun is made up of Darkness,

ness, and that Beauty itself is a Complication of Deformity and Horror.

When Mr. Pope penned the following Verses (in which the *philosophic* Inferences from the Doctrine of Necessity are summed up with equal Truth and Elegance), I cannot bring myself to suppose, that the Poet was in a *chearless, melancholy* Frame of Mind. So far from being able to observe the remotest Vestige of *Gloom*; I see nothing in them, but the Lustre of unmingled Light, and the Triumph of exulting Joy.

" Submit. — In this or any other Sphere,
Secure to be as Blest as thou canst bear.
Safe in the Hand of one Disposing Pow'r,
Or in the natal or the mortal Hour.
　All Nature is but Art, unknown to thee.
All Chance, Direction which thou canst not see.
All * Discord, Harmony not understood.
All partial Evil, universal Good.
And, spite of Pride, in erring Reason's Spight,
One Truth is clear: *Whatever* IS, *is* RIGHT."

If, together with the *philosophic*, we view Necessity through the *evangelic*, Medium; nothing will be wanting to render the Survey complete.

* All *Discord*, i. e. all the seemingly irregular and contrarient Dispensations of Divine Providence.

Christian Necessitarians, having sung with Mr. Pope; can *also* sing, as follows, in those chearfull Lines of the late excellent Mr. Hart:

" This God is the God we adore;
  Our faithfull, unchangeable Friend:
Whose Love is as great as His Pow'r,
  And knows neither Measure, nor End.

" 'Tis Jesus, the First and the Last,
  Whose Spirit shall guide us safe home!
We'll *praise* Him, for *All* that is past;
  And *trust* Him, for *All* that's to come."

And so much for the pretended GLOOMINESS of Necessity. Or, in other Words, for the *Æthiopic* Complection of that *dismal, melancholy* Doctrine, which most *dolefully* asserts, that *all Things*, without excepting the worst, *Work together* for the GLORY of GOD, and *for* GOOD *to them that love Him*. Rom. viii. 28. " Dri-plorable News indeed," as an old Lady once expressed it.

2. To shew his skill in History and Genealogy, Mr. Wesley traces the *Origin* of Necessity. And thus he makes out the Pedigree.

" That Man is not Self-determined; that the
" Principle of Action is lodged not in himself,
" but in some other Being; has been an *exceeding*

" *ing antient* Opinion: yea, near as old as the
" Foundation of the World. It seems, none
" that admit of Revelation can have any Doubt
" of this. For it was unquestionably the Senti-
" ment of *Adam*, soon after he had eaten of the
" forbidden Fruit. He imputes what he had
" done, not to himself, but another: *the Woman
" whom thou gavest me.* It was also the Senti-
" ment of *Eve: the Serpent, he beguiled me, and
" I did eat.* It is true, I did eat, but the Cause
" of my eating, the Spring of my Action, was
" in another."

Waiving all Notice of the grammatical and the logical Inaccuracys, which adorn this Paragraph; I shall, with it's Author's Leave, carry the *Antiquity* of Necessity somewhat higher up.

God Himself is a *necessary* Being. He existed, and *could not but* exist, without Beginning. He exists, and *cannot but* exist, without End. Necessity, therefore, is co-æval with, and inseparable from, Deity; i. e. it is, truly and properly, eternal: as all His other Attributes are. I would term Necessity, in this View of it, *Necessitas prima*.

With regard to *Adam*, he was sufficiently instructed in the Doctrine of Necessity, during the State of Innocence. He could not but know, that he existed necessarily, and that every Circumstance

cumstance of his Situation was necessarily determined by a superior Hand.

For Example. When he was well awoke from that *deep sleep*, into which he had been *necessarily* cast, without his own Consent first had and obtained; was not that single Incident (especially when he adverted to the important *Effect* of it) more than enough, to impress a reflecting Mind with the Idea of Necessity? The very missing of his *Rib*, which he had involuntarily lost on the Occasion; must have made him a Necessitarian, supposing him to have been, what I make no Doubt he was, a Man of common Understanding.

Eve, likewise, could not but know, that she was *necessarily* made, *necessarily* placed in Eden, and *necessarily* consigned to Adam.

I conclude, therefore, that the first Man and his Wife were Necessitarians, antecedently to their Fall. And if they, afterwards, endeavor'd to account for their Fall, upon the Principle of Necessity; I must declare, that, for my own Part, I see neither the Impiety of the Attempt, nor the Lameness of the Reasoning.

" Oh, but this makes God the Author of
" their Falling." By no Means in the World. 'Tis the *Arminian* Hypothesis, which represents Deity as either unseasonably *absent* from the Place, or as looking *unconcernedly* on, while His feeble
Creature

Creature Eve was chopping unequal Logic with a mightier and more artfull Being than herself. 'Tis the *Free-will* Scheme, which lays Original Sin at the Divine door: by supposing, that God stood *neuter* throughout the whole Affair; tho' He knew (if Arminianism will allow Him to have foreknown) that no less, than the Ruin of all Mankind, would be the Consequence of that Neutrality.

When we say, that the Fall of Man came *necessarily* to pass; 'tis only saying, that Satan is neither *too strong*, nor *too wise*, for God: and that Satan would not have proved too strong, or too wise, for Eve herself, had it been the Will of God *posuisse Obicem*, i. e. to have *hinder'd* Satan from succeding. Now, if 'twas *not* the Divine Will to *bar* the Enemy from succeding; and if it was really foreknown, that, without such Bar, the Enemy *would* succede; and if God could, without Injustice, actually *forbear*, at the very critical Time, to put an effectual Bar in the Way, though He certainly had Power to do it: the Inference is invincible, that Adam and Eve fell *necessarily*.

Nor is God's *Decree* to permit the Fall, liable to any one Cavil, which will not hold, with equal or with stronger Force, against *the actual Permission* itself. — " But *why* did God decree to
" permit

" permit the Fall, and permit the Fall according
" to His Decree?" For Reasons, the whole of
which He has not thought proper to communicate. *He giveth not Account, to Any, of His Matters.* Job. xxxiii. 13. And this is too good an Answer to so daring a Quæstion.

Let me give our Freewillers a very momentous Hint: viz. That the Entrance of Original Sin was one of those essential Links, on which the Messiah's Incarnation and Crucifixion were suspended. So that, if Adam's Fall was not *necessary* (i. e. if it was a *precarious*, or *contingent*, Event); it would follow, that the whole Christian Religion, from first to last, is a Piece of mere *Chance-medley*: and, consequently, cannot be of *Divine Institution*. Arminians would do well, to consider, whither their Principles lead them.

3. The true Necessity is, *toto Cælo*, remote and different from *Manichæism*: as indisputably appears, on comparing the two Systems together. Not to observe, that St. AUSTIN (who, in his earlier Part of Life, had been * entangled in the
Manichæan

---

* " The Manichæan Scheme," says Mr. *Wesley*, " was
" formerly espoused by Men of Renown: St Augustin in
" particular." But I will do St. Austin that Justice which this Gentleman witholds, by adding, that God converted him from Manichæism, while yet a young Man; and several
Years

Manichæan Net) was ultimately confirmed in his Refolution to renounce thofe Herefys, by reading the Epiftles of that illuftrious Neceffitarian St. *Paul.*

Manes, from whom Manichæifm is (though very inaccurately) denominated, was by Birth a Perfian, and florifhed toward the Clofe of the Third Century. His original Name was * *Cubric:* which

Years, before he was fo much as Baptized into the Chriftian Church. — The Methodift goes on. " Manichæifm is now " fo *utterly out of Date,* that it would be loft Labor to con-" fute it." Herein, he is, to expiefs it as tenderly as I can, *utterly miftaken in his Reckoning.* I fhall clearly prove, a page or two hence, that he himfelf is, in one Refpect, *as much;* and, in another Refpect, *abundantly more;* a *Manichæ,* than either Scythian, Budda, or Manes.

Mr. *Wefley,* by a very fingular Mixture of *Manichæifm, Pelagianifm, Popery, Socinianifm, Ranterifm,* and *Atheifm;* has, I believe, now got to his Ultimatum. Probably, he would go ftill farther, if he could. But, I really think, he has no farther to go. Happy Settlement, after Forty Years Infinity of Shiftings and Flittings hither and thither!

" Thus Weathercocks, which, for a while,
" Have turn'd about with ev'ry Blaft;
" Grown old, and deftitute of Oil,
" Ruft to a Point, and fix at laft!"

* " Mutato Nomine, deinde *Manis,* vel *Manetis,* Nomen adoptavit; Perficum aliis, quod ὁμιλητην dicat, *Difceptatorem, Agoniftam:*

which he afterwards dropped, for That of Manes.

One *Scythian*, an Arabian Merchant, who had made himself Master of the Oriental Philosophy and Theology, committed the Substance of his Collections to Writing: and bequeathed his Books, which were four in Number, to a Proselyte of his, named *Budda-Terebinthus*. This Budda, settling afterwards in Persia, resided in the House of a Widow, who had bought *Manes* for a Slave. On Budda's Decease, the Books of Scythian fell into Manes's Hands; from whence he drew the Generality of those Tenets which pass under his Name, and molded them into a System. In this odd Manner, did *Manes* come to distinguish himself as an Hæresiarch.

The Amount of his System was This.

' There

Agonistam: aliis Chaldaïcum מאני, Græcè μανης, ex מאן, quod, Babyloniorum Linguâ, significat, *Vas, Organum*; quòd se σκευ۞- εκλεκίον dicerat, quo Deus, ad Doctrinæ Divinæ Propagationem, uti vellet. Hinc videtur factum, ut falsæ Doctrinæ Auctorem Talmudistæ vocarint מיני; quod Elias Levita à מאן Hæretico derivat. Et reverà priùs Nomen *Cubricus* denotasse videtur כבו רין, *Vas vanum*, contemnendum, fragile. Dein Discipuli, ob Invidiam Græcæ Vocis, quâ Μανης designabat τον μαινονία τας φρενας, *insanentem*, vel *furentem*; Literâ duplicatâ, & compositâ Voce, quasi esset μαννα χεων, *Manna fundens*, fecere *Manichæum*."

Spanhemii Hist. Christian. Sæc. 3.—Operum Tom. I. Col. 751, 752.

' There are *two* co-æqual, co-æternal, and in-
' dependent *Gods,* or Infinite Principles: viz.
' *God,* properly so called; alias, Light: and
' *Matter*; alias, Darkness.

' The *First* is the Author of all *Good:* the Se-
' cond, of all *Evil.*

' The *light* God inspired the Penmen of the
' *New* Testament: the *dark* God inspired the
' Writers of the *Old* Testament. Consequently,
' the Old Testament is worth nothing.

' These Gods are real Substances: the one, a
' *good* Substance; the other, a *bad.*

' In the Work of Creation, the good Being
' wrought Part, and the bad Being wrought
' Part.

' The good Being is the Maker of human
' Souls.

' The good Being united himself to the Ele-
' ments of Air and Fire: the bad Being took
' Possession of Earth and Water.

' The evil God made the World, and the
' human Body, and Sin, and Magistracy.

' There is a Trinity: but it consists of *Scythian,*
' *Budda,* and *Manes.* Scythian's Seat is in the
' Sun: Budda's in the Moon: and Manes's in
' the Air.

' The Sun in the Firmament is Christ.

'. Christ

' Chrift did not affume a real, but only a *feem-*
' *ing* Body.

' The *Elect* are thofe, in whom the *evil* Prin-
' ciple is *quite done away*.

' *Matrimony* does but unite us more clofely to
' the evil God.

' Water-*Baptifm* is worth little.

' The Souls of my *Auditors'* [i. e. of thofe
who conftantly attended his Affemblys, and im-
bibed his Doctrines] ' are thereby changed into
' Elect Souls; and fo return, quite purify'd, to
' the good Being.

' The Souls of other People tranfmigrate, at
' Death, into *Beafts*, and *Trees*, and all Kinds of
' *Vegetables*.

' Inward Concupifcence is a *Perfon*. It is never
' *healed*, but it may be *totally feparated* from
' Men. In the Day of Judgement, each Con-
' cupifcence fhall be fhut up in a Globe, and there
' live in perpetual Imprifonment.

' The good God, and the bad God, wage im-
' placable and never ceafing War againft each
' other; and perpetually clog and difconcert one
' another's Schemes and Operations.

' Hence, Men are *impelled*, by *forcible* con-
' ftraint, to good, or to evil; according as they
' come under the Power of the good Deity, or the
' bad one.'

Such

Such is a Sketch of what I have been able to collect with Certainty, of the abfurd and execrable Tenets of *Manes:* which form a Medley of Pythagorifm, Gnofticifm, and almoft every other *ifm*, both Pagan and Hæretical, which that and præceding Ages could fupply. 'Tis probable, that *Budda* improved upon *Scythian*, and that *Manes* improved upon both. Tho', in Reality, neither of the Three, nor all the Three together, were *Authors* of the monftrous Opinions which conftituted the Jumble. The Opinions were taken from a Variety of other Sources: and the pilfering Triumvirate, contrary to the Practice of Thieves in general, feemed refolved to fteal the *worft* of every Thing they could lay their Hands on.

I believe, it is abfolutely impoffible to trace, quite up to it's Source, the Antiquity of that Hypothefis, which abfurdly affirms the Exiftence of *two eternal, contrary, independent Principles*. The other Oriental Nations feem to have adopted it from Egypt. But *whence* the Egyptians had it, and *when* they firft entertained it, we know not: at leaft, I could never find out.

What led fo many wife People, and for fo great a Series of Ages, into fuch a wretched Miftake; were, chiefly, I fuppofe, thefe two Confiderations: (1). That *Evil*, both moral and phyfical,

are

are *positive* Things, and so must have a positive Cause.—(2.) That a Being, *perfectly good*, could not, from the very Nature of His Essence, be the Cause of such *bad* Things.

But (1.) *Evil*, whether physical or moral, does not, upon a narrow Inspection, appear to have *so much* of *Positivity* in it, as 'tis probable those Antients supposed.

A Man breaks his Leg: i. e. the Continuity, or Co-hæsion of Parts, natural to that Limb, *ceases* to be integral. This is followed by the Evil of *Pain*. And what is Pain? the *Absence*, or *Privation*, of sensible Ease antecedently enjoy'd. —A Man's House is burned down. The Consequence is, a *Loss*, or *Privation*, of Property. He does *not* possess as much as he possess'd before. —Thus (not to multiply needless Instances), Sickness is a *Privation* of Health: and is, from thence, very properly termed, *Disease*. Poverty is a *Deficiency* of Wealth and Conveniences. Death itself, a *Cessation* of animal Life.

God forbid, that I should even wish to extenuate the Malignity of *Sin*. The omnipresent Reader of Hearts and Hearer of Thoughts knows, that, next after His own awefull Displeasure, I dread and deprecate Sin, in all it's Forms, as the greatest of possible Calamitys.—Let us, however,

with

with cautious and timid Hand, put Moral Evil itfelf into the philofophic Scale.

When I was a Boy, and began to read Watts's Logic, I well remember the Surprize it gave me, to find, that fo good a Man fhould venture to treat of *Sin*, in the 6th Section (Pt. 1. Chap. 2.), under the Title *Of Not-Being*. And, I confefs, I partly wonder at it ftill. But let the Doctor fpeak for himfelf. " The *Sinfullnefs* of any human Action " is faid to be a *Privation*: for Sin is that *Want* " of Conformity to the Law of God, which ought " to be found in every Action of Man. — — I " think," adds the Doctor, and in Troth I think fo too, " we muft not reduce fuch *pofitive* Beings " as *Piety*, and *Virtue*, and *Truth*, to the Rank " of *Non-entitys*, which have nothing real in " them. Though *Sin*, or rather the *Sinfullnefs* " of an Action, may be properly called a *Not-* " *Being*: for it is a *Want* of Piety and Virtue. " This is the moft ufual, and perhaps the moft " juft, Way of reprefenting thefe Matters."

Very happily, we have a Definition of Sin, given us by a Logician who could not err. Πας ὁ ποιων την ἁμαρτιαν, και την ανομιαν ποιει· και 'η ΑΜΑΡΤΙΑ ἐϛιν 'η ΑΝΟΜΙΑ. 1 John iii. 4. *Every Man, who committeth Sin, doth alfo commit Illegality: for* Sin *is* Illegality.—Whence I conclude, in the *firft* place: that Sin, ftrictly confider'd, has *more* of

K   Negation

Negation in it, that of Positivity; else, it could not have been properly defineable by a *merely negative* Term. For, *Illegality* imports no more, than a *Non-Commensuration* to the Law, as a Rule, or Measure of Length and Breadth.—But, *Secondly*, I infer, that, unless Sin had something of Positivity in it, the *Illegality* of it could not be said to be *commissable*: " Every Man, who com-" mitteth *Illegality*." And yet, after all, I do not *clearly* discern, how that can be, without the Assistance of Dr. *Watts*'s Distinction (a Distinction which is, I believe, admitted by most, if not all, metaphysical Writers) between *Actions* themselves, and the *Sinfullness* of them.

Critics explain פשע, one of the Hebrew Words for *Sin*, by the Greek Word αθεσια; which imports *Unsettledness*, and, in particular, a *not standing* to Articles before agreed upon. חטא, the most usual Word for Sin, properly signifys, a *not walking* in the right Road, and a *not hitting* the proposed Mark. עון is *Obliquity*, or *Crookedness*: i. e. *Want* of Straitness.

The Greek αμαρτια, most certainly, conveys a negative Idea: and signifys, like the second Hebrew Word abovemention'd, a *falling short* of the Mark.

The Latin *Peccatum* (which some are for deriving from פשע) is also explained by *Delictum*, i. e. a *Failure* a *Failure* in Duty. *Iniquitas, Culpa, Noxa, Injuſtitia, Impietas, Scelus, Vitium,* and a Multitude of others; are, in Strictneſs, Terms of Negation.

But (2.), in what Light ſoever we conſider thoſe Modes of Being and of Action, called natural and moral Evil; whether we view them as poſitive Qualitys, or as negative, or as mixed; ſtill the Quæſtion returns, *Whether the Great* First Cause, *who is infinitely and merely Good, can be, either* efficiently, *or* deficiently, *the Author of them?*

In my Opinion, the ſingle Word *Permiſſion* ſolves the whole Difficulty, as far as it can be ſolved in the preſent beclouded State of human Reaſon. Certainly, God is *not bound* to præclude Evil from among His Works. 'Tis equally certain, that He *can* permit it, not only to obtain, but even to reign. And 'tis as certain, that He actually *does* ſo permit it. Why? Not for Want of *Knowledge,* to perceive it. Nor for Want of *Power,* to hinder it. Nor for Want of *Wiſdom,* to counteract it. Nor for Want of *Goodneſs,* to order all for the beſt. But becauſe it was and is His unſearchable * *Will* (and the Will of God is Rectitude

---

* And a Step, or an Inch, beyond *this,* we cannot go. That God *willed* to permit Evil, cannot be doubted; but at the

Rectitude itfelf), to allow the Entrance and the Continuance of that feeming Foil to the Lovelinefs of His Works,

Arminianifm

the Expence, either of His Wifdom, or of His Power. The Reafons *why* He willed it, are, perhaps, among thofe Arcana, which Angels themfelves have not yet been allowed to fee into.

I think, I may venture to affert, that the Scriptures throw hardly any Degree of Light upon the Divine *Motive*, or Motives, to this Permiffion. And it appears inconteftably plain, from the Writings, and from fuch authentic Memorials, as remain, of the moft fagacious Philofophers of præceding Ages, and of every civilized Clime, the *Chinefe* themfelves included; that all their various Hypothefes (fome of which were extremely fubtil and ingenious), by which they ftrained both Judgement and Imagination, to account for the primary Exiftence and Introduction of moral and phyfical Ataxy; terminated, univerfally, in the Point from whence they fat out: viz. *We cannot tell.*

Whoever defires to fee, at one View, as much as needs to be known, concerning the Speculations of the greateft Sages among the Antients, on this inextricable Subject; will enjoy a moft refined Amufement (but attended, I think, with no feafible Solution of the Difficulty immediately in Point), by perufing the fecond Part of that concife, elegant, judicious, and faithfull Sketch of antique Philofophy, entitled; *A Difcourfe upon the Theology and Mythology of the Antients.* Written by the Chevalier *Ramfay:* an Author, who, tho', in my Opinion, extremely fancifull and erroneous on fome metaphyfical Quæftions; yet deferves to be lov'd and admired, as one of the moft ingenious, polite, candid, and entertaining

Arminianifm (which reprefents moral and natural Evil as entering and as reigning in DEFIANCE and

tertaining Reafoners, that ever added the Enchantments of Beauty to the Dignity of Virtue and to the Riches of Learning.

But ftill, our utmoft Inveftigations leave us, præcifely, where they began. We know fcarce any of the Views, which induced Uncreated Goodnefs to ordain (for, where Infinity of Knowledge and of Power and of Wifdom unite in the Permittor, I fee no very great Difference between *permitting* and *ordaining*) the Introgreffion, or, more properly, the Intromiffion, of Evil. For my own Part, I can, with unrepining Chearfullnefs, give God Credit (and that to all Eternity, fhould it be His Pleafure to require me) for doing every Thing well.

" I know but this, that He is good,
" And that myfelf am blind."

Can any body bring the Matter to a more fatisfactory Iffue? *Si non, hoc utere mecum.*

It might have been happy for that fine, but too excurfive Theorift, Dr. *Conyers Middleton*; if he had not, with more Rafhnefs than good Speed, endeavor'd to overleap that Boundary, which God Himfelf has fixed, to the prefent Extent of human Knowledge. Were we even to grant the Doctor his favorite Hypothefis, viz. that the *whole* Mofaic Account of the Fall is *merely allegorical*; the Origin of Evil would ftill remain as dark, and as deep at the Bottom of the Well, as ever. For to what does this boafted Allegory amount? Dr. Middleton fhall give it us, in his own Words (*Works*, Quarto. Vol. II. P. 149). " By ADAM, we are to
" underftand

and Contrariety to the *Will* and *Wish* and *Endeavors* of the Divine Being) co-incides so patly

" understand *Reason*, or the Mind of Man. By Eve, the
" *Flesh*, or outward Senses. By the Serpent, *Lust*, or Plea-
" sure. In which Allegory, we see clearly explained the
" true Causes of Man's Fall and Degeneracy: that, as soon
" as his Mind, thro' the Weakness and Treachery of his
" Senses, became captivated and seduced by the Allure-
" ments of Lust and Pleasure; he was driven by God out
" of Paradise, i. e. lost and forfeited the Happiness and
" Prosperity, which he had enjoy'd in his Innocence."

With all the Respect due to so very superior a Pen, I would offer an Observation or two on this Passage.—1. If *Adam*, and *Eve*, and the *Serpent*, and the *Trees* of Knowledge and of Life, and the very *Paradise* where they grew, were all allegorical (i. e. fabulous and unreal); might not an Atheist suppose, with equal Reason, that the adorable Creator, whom this same History terms God, is as allegorical a Being as the rest?—2. If the *Fall* itself, as related in Scripture, be no more than a Piece of moral Fiction; what Security have we, that the scriptural Account of *Redemption*, is not equally fictitious? Indeed, where is the Necessity, or so much as the Propriety, and Reasonableness, of imagining, that an allegorical Ruin requires more than an allegorical Restoration?—3. Among a Multitude of other Objections, which clog the Wheel of this unsatisfactory Scheme; the following is one: that the Difficulty of *accounting* for the Rise of Evil, still subsists in all it's primitive and impenetrable Obscurity. For, (1.) How came the " Allurements of Lust and Plea-
" sure," to exist at all? especially, in a State of absolute Innocency?—(2.) How came Man's " outward Senses" to

be

patly with the *Manichæan* Dream of *two almighty conflicting Principles*, who reign in spight of each other, and catch as Catch can; that I really wonder at the reversed modesty of those Free-willers, who are for shifting off the Charge of Manichæism, from themselves, to other Folks.

be so very easy of Access, as to fly open, like the Doors of an enchanted Castle, at almost the first Appearance of this said gigantic Lady, called " Allurement"?—(3.) How came the Human Mind to yield itself so tame a " Captive" to those seducing senses? Not to ask, (4.) Why the Senses themselves were originally indued with that " Weakness, " and Treachery," and Power of " Seduction," which the Doctor so freely places to their Account?—I think myself warranted to conclude, that this masterly Allegorizer has NOT " clearly explaned", nor so much as thrown the least Glimmering of Explanation upon, " the true Causes of " Man's Fall and Degeneracy". What, then, do we gain, by reading Moses through the Doctor's allegoric Spectacles? So far from gaining, we lose the little we had. The Man who pulls down my House, and builds me a better in it's Place; deserves my thanks. But the Man who takes down my Dwelling, under Pretence that it is not sufficiently ample and elegant for a Person of my Dignity to inhabit; and, after all this Parade, leaves me to sleep in the open Air, unshelter'd by any Roof at all: does me a material Injury. When Infidels can raise a more commodious Fabric (i. e. propose a more unexceptionable System of Principles), than That the Bible presents us with; we'll chearfully remove from our old House. But, 'till then, let those Gentlemen sleep *sub Dio* by themselves.

Nay, were I difpofed to make the moft of my Argument, I might add, and very fairly too, That the old Manichæifm was a *gentle* Impiety, and a *flender* Abfurdity; when contrafted with the modern Arminian Improvements on that Syftem. For, which is worfe? To affert the Exiftence of *two* independent Beings, and no more; or, To affert the Exiftence of about *One Hundred and Fifty Millions* of independent Beings, all living at one Time, and moft of them waging fuccefs-full War on the Defigns of Him that made them?

Moreover, if fo very minute a Crumb of the Creation, as this terraqueous Planet, which we at prefent occupy, can furnifh out fuch a formidable Army of independent Principles (i. e. of *Self-determiners:* in which Number, Infants and Children themfelves muft be virtually included, which will fwell the Catalogue with about Seventy Millions more); the aggregate Number of independent and poffibly-conflicting Agents, contained in the Univerfe at large, may excede the Powers of all the Angels in Heaven to compute. But, even confining ourfelves to our own World; it will follow, that *Arminian* Manichæifm EXCEDES the paltry *Oriental* Duality, at the immenfe Rate of 150000000 to 2! And this, at the very loweft and moft favorable Computation, i. e. without

taking

taking Infants into the Account; and without reckoning the adult Self-determiners of *past* Generations, nor of those Generations which are yet *to come.*

Poor *Manes!* with how excellent a grace do ARMINIANS call *thee* an Heretic! And, above all, *such* Arminians (whereof Mr. *John Wesley* is one) as agree with thee, in believing the Attainability of *sinless Perfection* here below: or, to use the good old *Manichæan* Phrase, who assert that *The* EVIL *Principle may be* TOTALLY SEPARATED *from Man in the present Life!*

" Oh, but Manes held *Necessity* also." But what *Sort* of Necessity? Such a Necessity as a Child would be under, if the Dragon of Wantley was pulling him by one Arm, and Moore of Moore-hall by the other. Christianity and Philosophy have nothing to do with *this* Necessity, except to laugh at it.

4. Mr. Wesley seems much displeased with a Brace of Gentlemen, whose Names he has not communicated to the Public; but who appear, from his Account of 'em, to be in no very fair Way toward *sinless Perfection.*

One of these, we are told, deliver'd his Mind, to this Effect: " I frequently feel Tempers, and " speak many Words, and do many Actions, " which I don't approve of. But I cannot avoid
" it,

" it. They refult, whether I will or no, from
" the Vibrations of my Brain, together with the
" Motion of my Blood, and the Flow of my
" animal Spirits. But thefe are not in my own
" Power. I cannot help them. They are inde-
" pendent on my Choice." Thus far, I totally
agree with the Gentleman unknown. Every one
of his Præmiffes is true. But the Conclufion
limps, moft miferably. Which Conclufion (if
Mr. Wefley have reprefented it fairly) is this:
" Therefore I cannot apprehend myfelf to be a
" *Sinner.*" And pray, what *does* the Gentleman
apprehend himfelf to be? A *Saint*, I prefume.
Should this Tract ever fall into his Hands, let
me intreat him to cry mightily to God, for that
fupernatural Influence of Grace, which alone is
able to *convince* him of his Sinnerfhip; to *bring*
him to Chrift; and to *fave* him from the evil
Effects, which muft, otherwife, continue to refult
from " the Vibrations of his Brain, the Motion
" of his Blood, and the Flow of his animal
" Spirits."

The other anonymous Gentleman, according
to Mr. Wefley's Hiftory of him, believes the
Omnipotence, but doubts the *Wifdom*, and flatly
denys the *Goodnefs*, of God. From the peculiar
Complection of this Creed, I fhould have
imagined, that it's Compiler had picked up the

two

two laſt Articles of it at the Foundery: but Mr. Weſley præcludes this Surmiſe, by giving us to underſtand, that the Gentleman is not a Free-willer. For thus the Creed goes on: " All the " Evil in the World is owing to God. I can " aſcribe it to no other Cauſe. I cannot blame " that Cur, for barking or biting: it is his " Nature: and he did not make himſelf. I feel " wrong Tempers in myſelf. But that is not " *my* Fault: for I cannot help it. It is my " Nature. And I could not *prevent* my having " this Nature: neither can I *change* it."

No Man in the World is more prone to put Things in People's Mouths, which they never ſaid, or thought of, than Mr. *J. W.* I therefore lay very little Streſs on the Teſtimony, which ſupports the Authenticity of this Creed. It *may* be genuine. But 'tis more probable, that 'twas *forged*, and dreſſed up, for the Occaſion.

However, I will beſtow a few conciſe Annotations on this Confeſſion of Faith, be it real, or be it fictitious.

' *All the Evil in the World is* owing *to God.*' Nothing can be more falſe. For, as the great and good Mr. * Edwards obſerves, " It would be
" ſtrange

* Viz. the late Rev. Mr. *Jonathan Edwards*, of North America, Whoſe *Enquiry into the Freedom of the Will* is a
Book

"strange arguing indeed, becaufe Men never
"commit Sin, but only when God leaves them
"*to*

Book which God has made the Inftrument of more deep and extenfive Ufefullnefs (efpecially among Deifts, and Perfons of Science), than almoft any other modern Publication I know of. If fuch of my Readers, as have not yet met with it, wifh to fee the *Arminian* Sophiftry totally unravel'd and defeated; let 'em add that excellent Performance to their literary Treafures. A more nervous Chain of Reafoning it would be extremely difficult to find, in the *Englifh* Language. Confequently, it is not one of thofe Treatifes, that can be run through in an Hurry. It muft be read deliberately, and weighed with Attention: elfe, you'll lofe half the Strength of the Connection.——A fpruce Maccaroni was boafting, one Day, that He had the *moft happy Genius* in the World. *Every thing*, faid he, *is eafy to me*. People call Euclid's *Elements an hard Book: but I read it, Yefterday, from Beginning to End, in a Piece of the Afternoon, between Dinner and Tea-time*. " Read all Euclid," anfwered a Gentleman prefent, " in one Afternoon? How was that poffible?" *Upon my Honor, I did: and never read more fmoother reading in my Life*. " Did you mafter all the Demonftrations, and folve " all the Problems, as you went?" *Demonftrations! and Problems! I fuppofe you mean the* a*'s, and* b*'s, and* c*'s; and the* 1*'s, and* 2*'s, and* 3*'s; and the Pictures of Scratches and Scrawls. No, No. I fkipt all they. I only read* Euclid *himfelf; and* ALL *Euclid I* DID *read; and in one Piece of the Afternoon too*.— Mr. Edward's muft not be read fo genteelly.

There are, it feems, two eminent Defences of Neceffity, which I have never yet feen; viz. Dr. Hartley's *Obferva-*
tions

" *to themselves*, and neceſſarily Sin, when He
" does ſo; that therefore their Sin is *not from
" themſelves*, but from God: and ſo, that God
" muſt be a ſinfull Being. As ſtrange, as it
" would be, to argue, becauſe it is always dark
" when the Sun is gone, and never dark when
" the Sun is preſent; that therefore all Darkneſs
" is from the Sun, and that his Diſk and Beams
" muſt needs be black." (*Enquiry*, P. 364,
365.)

Mr. *Weſley*'s Neceſſitarian adds: ' *I cannot
* BLAME *that Cur for barking and biting.*' But
did the Gentleman never, ſo much as once in his
Life time, *beat* a Cur for barking and biting?
I dare ſay, he has: and would again, if a Cur
was to fly at him with open Mouth. It ſhould
ſeem, therefore, that a Cur, tho' he bark and
bite *neceſſarily*, is liable ſtill to *Blame:* elſe, how
could he be juſtly entitled to *Blows*?

' *It is his Nature.*' Moſt certainly. And yet
you'll *beat* him for it!

' *He did not make himſelf.*' Who thinks he
did?

---

tions on Man; and an anonymous *Eſſay on Liberty and Ne-
ceſſity*, publiſhed, ſome Years ſince, at Edinburgh. I hope,
I have a Feaſt, of Pleaſure and Inſtruction, in Reſerve.
And it ſhall not be my Fault, if I do not ſoon enjoy it.

' *I feel*

'*I feel wrong Tempers in myself.*' I dare say, You do.

'*But that is not* MY *Fault.*' Certainly, the Fault's *in* Yourself; and, consequently, the Fault is *your*'s. How you came by it, is another Matter: and belongs to the Quæstion of Original Sin.

'*I cannot help it.*' Right: *you* cannot. But there is ONE that can. Apply to Him.

'*It is my Nature.*' Very true.—'*And I could not* PREVENT *my having this Nature.*' I never imagined you could.——'*Neither can I* CHANGE '*it.*' I am very clear, you cannot. The Æthiopian might as soon change his Skin, or the Leopard his Spots, Jer. xiii. 23. And yet, what will become of you, if you dye *unchanged?* May the Almighty put that Cry into your Heart, *Turn* THOU *me, and I* SHALL *be turned; for Thou art the Lord my God.* Jer. xxxi. 18. Then will you know what This meaneth: *We all, with open Face, beholding, as in a Glass, the Glory of the Lord;* ARE CHANGED *into the same Image, from Glory to Glory, by the Spirit of the Lord.* 2 Cor. iii. 18.

5. Mr. Wesley's Wrath is not confined to the two Gentlemen abovemention'd. It strides back into the last Century, and prosecutes " The " *Assembly of Divines* who met at *Westminster.*" For what Offence, are they thus dug out of their Graves?

Graves? For saying, that "Whatever happens "in Time, was unchangeably determined from "all Eternity."— I beg Leave to acquaint the Court, that there's a Flaw in the Charge. Mr. Wesley cannot quote even a single Proposition, without *mangling* and *altering!*

In the Confession, drawn up by those Divines, they express the Matter thus: *God, from all Eternity, did, by the most wise and holy Counsel of His own Will, freely and unchangeably ordain whatsoever comes to pass. Yet so, as thereby neither is God the Author of Sin, nor is Violence offer'd to the Will of the Creatures,* &c. *.— In their larger Catechism, they phrase it, with no Alteration of Sense, as follows: *God's Decrees are the wise, free, and holy Acts of the Counsel of His Will; whereby, from all Eternity, He hath, for His own Glory, unchangeably fore-ordained whatsoever comes to pass in Time: especially, concerning Angels and Men.* — In the shorter Catechism, they say: *The Decrees of God are, His Eternal Purpose according to the Counsel of his Will; whereby, for His own Glory, He hath fore-ordained whatever comes to pass. God executeth His Decrees, in the Works of Creation and Providence.*— I shall only observe,

---

* Humble Advice of the Assembly, &c. P. 10, 11.— Edit. Lond. 1658. Quarto.

concerning all and each of thefe Paragraphs, that if they be not true, the whole Bible is one grand ftring of Falfehood, from the firft Verfe to the laft.

While Mr. Wefley's hand was in, I wonder he did not arraign *another* Affembly of Divines; fome of whom were *Mitred*. I mean, the famous Affembly of Bifhops and others, who met together, not many Bow-fhots from Weftminfter, on the Surrey Side of the Thames, in the Year 1595, at a certain Place of Rendezvous, called *Lambeth Palace:* where, fays Dr. Fuller, " Arch-" Bifhop *Whitgift*, out of his CHRISTIAN CARE " to propagate the TRUTH, and *fupprefs* the " oppofite ERRORS, caufed a folemn Meeting of " many grave and learned Divines." Among whom, befides the good Arch-Bifhop himfelf, were *Bancroft*, Bp. of London; *Vaughan*, Bp. of Bangor; *Tindal*, Dean of Ely; *Whitaker*, Divinity Profeffor of Cambridge; &c. Which faid *Affembly of Divines* drew up the celebrated LAMBETH ARTICLES: whereof I fhall here cite but one, for a Specimen; having treated, at large, of this Affembly, and it's Determinations, * elfewhere, " Prædeftinatorum præfinitus et certus

---

* In a Tract, entitled, *The Church of England vindicated from the Charge of Arminianifm*; and in my *Hiftoric Proof of the Doctrinal Calvinifm of the Church of England*.

eft

" eft Numerus: qui nec augeri, nec minui,
" poteſt." i. e. *The Number of the Prædeſtinated is fore-determined, and certain: ſo that it can neither be increaſed, nor diminiſh'd.*

There have alſo been ſtill *larger* Aſſemblys of Divines: eompoſed of all the Biſhops, Deans, and Delagates of the Clergy, in England. Witneſs the *Aſſembly*, who drew up the 39 Articles. Articles, to which Mr. *Weſley* has, indeed, over and over again, ſat his Hand: but with the ſame *Simplicity* and *godly Sincerity* (2 Cor. i. 12.), which ſeem to have actuated Dr. *Reid*, Dr. *Oſwald*, and Dr. *Beattie*, when they ſubſcribed The Confeſſion and Catechiſm of the Weſtminſter Aſſembly.

There's ſuch a Thing, as holy Tricking.
Teſts are but Pye-cruſt, made for breaking.
Our own Conveniency, and Gains,
Are Sweetmeats, which that Cruſt contains.
To come at theſe, what Man ſo fooliſh,
But would a thouſand Cruſts demoliſh?

Moreover, what ſhall we ſay, concerning that Moſt Reverend, Right Reverend, and Reverend, *Aſſembly*; who put that woefull Collect into the Liturgy, beginning with, O God, *whoſe never-*

never-failing Providence ordereth ALL *Things, both in Heaven and Earth?* Can any Thing breathe, more strongly, the whole of what we mean by NECESSITY? — A *Providence* — a *never-failing Providence* — that *ordereth*, not only some, but *all* Things — Yea, all Things both in *Heaven* and *Earth!* In that one Passage (and the Church has very many others, quite like unto it), " See " *Necessity* drawn at full Length, and painted in " the most lively Colors"!

6. 'Tis curious, to behold *Arminians* themselves forced, by Stress of Argument, to take Refuge in the Harbor of that *Necessity* which, at other Times, they so vehemently seek to destroy. " It " is *necessary*," say they, " that Man's Will should " be *free:* for, without Freedom, the Will were " no Will at all."

I pity the distressfull Dilemma, to which they are driven. Should they say, it is *not* necessary for Man's Will to be free; they give up their whole Cause at once. If they say (and say it they do), that it *is* necessary, yea *absolutely* necessary, for the Will to be free; and that, in it's very Nature, it *cannot but* be free; — then, say I, upon that Principle, these good People are free, with *a Liberty of Necessity*, and shere Necessity itself is the Root and Sap of all their boasted

Free-

Free-Agency. In other Words, *Free-Agency*, themselves being Judges, is only *a Ramification of* NECESSITY!

7. Tho' I have mention'd the following Anecdote, in a præceding Publication; yet, by way of recompensing Mr. Wesley, for the Amusement he has afforded me, in publishing the Conversations of the two *necessitarian Gentlemen*, whereof I have just given the Reader an Account; I also, in my Turn, shall refer him to a very remarkable Conversation, which passed between a *Free-will Gentleman* and myself, June 21, 1774, in the Neighborhood of London, and in the Presence of my Friend, the Rev. Mr. Ryland.

" God does all He POSSIBLY CAN", said the Arminian Philosopher, " to HINDER moral " and natural Evil. But He CANNOT PREVAIL. " Men will not PERMIT God to have His Wish." — *Then the Deity*, answer'd I, *must certainly be a very* UNHAPPY *Being.* — " Not unhappy in the " least." — *What! meet with a constant Series of crosses*; THWARTED *in his daily Endeavors*; DISAPPOINTED *of his Wishes*; DISCONCERTED *in his Plan of Operations*; DEFEATED *of his Intentions*; EMBARRASS'D *in his Views*; *and actually* OVERPOWER'D, *every Moment of every Day, by number-*

L 2

less

less of the Creatures He has made; and yet be HAPPY *under all this incessant Series of* PERPLEXING *and* MORTIFYING *Circumstances?* — " Yes: for
" He knows, that, in Consequence of the FREE-
" WILL, with which He has endu'd his rational
" Creatures, He Himself MUST be *disappointed*
" of his Wishes, and *defeated* of his Ends; and
" that *there is* NO HELP *for it*, unless He had
" made us mere Machines. He therefore SUB-
" MITS to *Necessity:* and does not make Himself
" uneasy about it *."

Can any Thing be more *shockingly execrable*, than such a degrading and blasphemous Idea of the Ever Blessed GOD? And, consequently, is not the Doctrine of *Human Self-Determinability* the most daring, the most inconsistent, the most false, the most contemptible, and the most atheistical Tenet, that was ever spawned by Pride and Ignorance in conjunction? A Doctrine, which, in running away from the *true* Necessity, coins an *impossible* Necessity of it's own inventing; and,

---

* See a Note, subjoined to P. 5. of a Sermon lately published by me, entitled, *Freewill and Merit brought to the Test*; or, *Men not their own Saviors:* where some of the horrible Consequences, and of the gigantic Inconsistencys, inseparable from this Gentleman's Theory, are briefly pointed out.

while

while it reprefents *Men* as *Gods*, finks GOD far below the Level of the meaneft *Man!*

Is not the adorable CREATOR of the World, the GOVERNOR of it too? Or has He only built a Stage, for *Fortune* to dance upon? Does ALMIGHTY PROVIDENCE do no more than hold the Diftaff, while *Contingency* (i. e. while *Nothing*) fpins the Threads, and wreathes them into a Line, for the FIRST CAUSE (very falfely fo called, if this be the Cafe!) to wind upon his Reel, and turn to the beft Account He can? Arminians may affirm it. But God forbid, that I fhould ever believe it.

For my own Part, I folemnly profefs, before God, Angels, and Men, that I am *not confcious* of my being endued with that Self-determining Power, which Arminianifm afcribes to me as an Individual of the Human Species. Nay, I am *clearly certain*, that I have it not. I am alfo equally certain, that I *do not wifh* to have it: and that, was it poffible for my Creator to make me an offer of transferring the Determination of any one Event, from His own Will to mine; it would be both my Duty and my Wifdom, to entreat, that the Sceptre might ftill remain with Himfelf, and that I might having nothing to do in the Direction of a fingle Incident, or of fo much as a fingle Circumftance.

Mr. Wesley laments, that *Necessity* is "The Scheme, which is now adopted by not a few of the most sensible Men in the Nation." I agree with him, as to the Fact. But I cannot deplore it as a Calamity. The Progress, which that Doctrine has, of late Years, made, and is still making, in this Kingdom; I consider as a most happy and promising Symptom, that the Divine Goodness has yet abundant Mercys in Reserve, for a *Church*, the Majority of whose reputed Members have long apostatized from her essential Principles; and for a *Country*, whose *

Morals

* Take a Specimen of the vitiated State, to which the *Free-will* Gangrene has reduced the *moral* Taste of this *Christian* and *Reformed* Country; in the following *admired* Lines, which are Part of a very *applauded* Entertainment, lately introduced on the English Stage:

" *With Sport, Love, and Wine, fickle* FORTUNE *defy.*
" DULL WISDOM *all Happiness sours.*
Since Life is no more than a Passage, AT BEST;
Let us strew the Way over with Flow'rs."

Was a religious and sensible Foreigner, whether Protestant, or Popish; Jew, Mahometan, or Heathen; to be informed, that such equally detestable and despicable Sentiments, as those, are heard with Rapture at the British Theatres, and chorus'd with Delight in numberless private Companys, in every Part of the Kingdom: would he not be inclined to set

us

Morals have degenerated, in Proportion to the Corruptions of it's Faith.

May *the* * *set Time* be nigh at Hand, for our National Recovery to the Gospel and to Virtue! Then shall God, even our own God, give us His Blessing.

us down, in general, for a Nation of Epicuræan Atheists, fit only to wallow in the Circæan Sty; quite lost to all Religion, Philosophy, Virtue, and Decency; and no otherwise entitled to the Name of Man, than by *Perpendicularity of Shape* connected with *the Art of Speaking?*

" If prone in Thought, our Stature is our Shame:
" And Man should blush, his Forehead meets the Skys."

* Psalm cii. 13.

A

DISSERTATION

CONCERNING THE

SENSIBLE QUALITYS

OF

MATTER:

MORE ESPECIALLY, CONCERNING

COLORS.

Judge not (κατ' ΟΨΙΝ) *according to Sight.* John vii. 24.

A DISSERTATION, &c.

WHEN I wrote the foregoing Chapters, it was my Intention to have taken no Notice of Mr. Wesley's weak and puerile Objections to the well established Doctrine of *sensible Qualitys:* partly, because what he observes (or, rather, what he has picked up from Dr. Reid and others) on this Subject, is so contemptibly frivolous, as hardly to justify any serious Animadversion; and, partly, because I did not consider the Subject itself as directly connected with the Article of Necessity.

But, on my reflecting, that the *Aptitude* of perceivable Bodys to impress our Senses with certain Motions, called Sensations; and that the *Sensations* so produced, together with the correspondent *Ideas* which those Sensations impart to, or excite

excite in, the Mind; are, All, the Result of necessary Relation, and form an indissolubly combined Chain of Cause and Effect: I determined to subjoin some Enquirys, concerning a Branch of Knowledge, which, in *this* View of it, is not altogether foreign to the main Argument of the præceding Disquisitions.

By the *Senses*, I mean those Conduits or Avenues to the Brain, through which, the Soul receives it's Ideas of Objects extraneous to it's Self. No Person need be reminded, that these Senses are five; viz. those of feeling, hearing, seeing, smelling, and tasting. — It may, perhaps, be solidly affirmed, that, in absolute Strictness, we have but *one* Sense, præcisely so called: viz. that of *Feeling*, or Perception at large; of which the remaining four are but so many exquisite Modifications, or Affections. I acquiesce, however, in the popular Division of the Senses into five.

The *sensible Qualitys* of extraneous Objects are, properly, no more than " *Powers,*" as Mr. Locke justly terms them; viz. Powers *of producing* such particular Motions in our animal Organs, as have a native Tendency to occasion correspondent Perceptions in the Soul, through the Mediation of the Nerves and Brain: that is to say, extraneous Objects have this *Effect*, when duly presented to the Senses, and when the Senses are in such a State

as

as duly to receive the Impreſſions naturally ariſing from the Preſence, or Application, of thoſe Objects.

Theſe Powers, inhærent in extraneous Bodys, of producing ſuch Senſations in Us; indiſputably reſult from the Figure, Size, Arrangement, and Motion, of the Particles which conſtitute the Bodys themſelves. Which appears, among other Conſiderations, from hence: that *the ſame Body*, under *different Modes* of corpuſcular Size, Arrangement, Motion, and Figure, occaſions *different Senſations* in our Organs, and conveys *different Ideas* to the Mind.

Now, theſe *modal Differences* of Arrangement, &c; are undoubtedly reſident in their reſpective Subjects: and may eaſily be conceived of, as exiſtible, *independently* on Us; i.e. they might be juſt what they are, whether the Bodys themſelves, in which they obtain, were objected to our Senſes, or not. But the EFFECTS of thoſe combined Modes (as Color, Sound, Flavor, Scent, Pleaſure, and Pain) are Things PURELY RELATIVE: and abſolutely require the Concurrence of *Senſe*, in order to their having any Kind or Degree of *poſitive* Exiſtence. They are but *potentially* in their peculiar Subjects, 'till thoſe Subjects become Objects, by being actually expoſed to, and by actually operating upon, the Organs of a percipient Being.

Thus,

Thus, there might have been Tremulations in the Atmosphære, through the Impulse of one Mass of Matter upon another (primarily set in Motion by the Divine Will), if no Animal, or sentient Being, had been created. But, in that Case, it is utterly inconceivable, how those Tremulations, tho' ever so violent, could have occasion'd what we call, *Sound.* — Again. The Disposition of certain Surfaces to reflect, refract, and absorb, the incident Rays of Light; might have been just what it now is, independently on the optic Nerves of Animals: but then no Surface, however disposed, i. e. be it's Texture, Reflections, Refractions, or Absorptions, what they will; could have occasioned that ideal Result, which we term *Color,* without being opposed to the visual Organ of an intelligent Substance. — And so on, through every Species of sensible Quality.

Hence, there is nothing hyperbolic, or extravagant; but all is no less strictly and soberly philosophical, than sublimely and elegantly poetical; in the following Lines of Dr. Young.

" The *Senses,* which inherit Earth and Heavens,
Enjoy the various Riches Nature yields:
Far nobler! *give* the Riches they enjoy.
Give Taste to Fruits; and Harmony to Groves;
The

The radiant Beams to Gold, and Gold's bright
    Sire:
Take in, at once, the Landscape of the World,
At a small Inlet, which a Grain might close,
And *half-create* the wondrous World they see.
But for the magic Organ's pow'rfull Charm,
Earth were a rude, uncolor'd Chaos still.
Objects are but th' *Occasion*: our's th' Exploit.
Our's are the Cloth, the Pencil, and the Paint,
Which Nature's admirable Picture draw,
And beautify Creation's ample Dome.
Like Milton's *Eve*, when gazing on the Lake,
Man makes the matchless Image, Man admires."

    This is provable, not only by Reason, but by numberless *Experiments*. Do but artfully vary the Medium through which you see it, and you may make the Surface of any Body whatever assume, in Appearance, any *Color* you please: and that in the most rapid Succession, and in every Mode of possible Diversity. A certain Sign, that Color is only a *sensible Quality*, and not a *real Property*, of Matter.

    But let us hear Mr. Wesley: who wildly thinks himself no less qualifyed to demolish the fundamental Axioms of Natural Philosophy, than to overturn the first Principles of Natural and Revealed Religion.

                                " '*Color*,"

" *Color*", fays he, " is a *real, material Thing*.
" There is no Illufion in the Cafe, unlefs you
" confound the * Perception with the * Thing
" perceived. And *all other* fecondary Qualitys
" are juft as *real*, as Figure, or any other
" Primary one." With Regard to *Color* (for I
have neither Room nor Leifure to run through
all the other fecondary Qualitys), it's non-exiftence is certain, not only from the præceding
Confiderations; but, likewife, in general, from the
natural Darknefs of Matter. Every Atom (even
thofe not excepted, which conftitute that exquifit
Fluid, called *Light*; tho' it is the moft attenuated
and fubtil Body with which we are acquainted)
is, intrinfecally, *dark:* and, confequently, *colorlefs.* Light itfelf, by whofe Intervention other
Bodys become vifible, feems to depend greatly,
if not entirely, for that Power, on the Exility,
the extreme Rarefaction, and on the incomparably
rapid Motion, Expanfion, and Protrudibility, of it's
component Particles: by which Propertys, it is

---

* * The plain, natural Meaning of this, is, that "*The Thing*
" *perceived*," viz. Color, confider'd as refident in Bodys, is
" *real:*" but that our " *Perception*" of that " *real*" Color
is a mere " *Illufion*"! — Without any " Illufion" at all, may
we not pronounce Mr. Wefley to be the lameft, the blindeft,
and the moft felf-contradictory Wafter of Ink and Paper, that
ever pretended to the Name of Reafoner? 'Tis almoft a Difgrace, to refute him.

peculiarly

peculiarly fitted, to act upon the Instruments of animal Sight; as these are likewise reciprocally fitted to admit that Sensation, which Providence designed they should receive, in Consequence of being so acted upon.

"All Colors," says Mr Wesley, " do as really " exist without us, as Trees, or Corn, or Heaven, " or Earth." He is welcome to enjoy a Delusion, which (like most of his other Opinions) has not one sound Argument for it's Support. But hear him again: " When I say, That Cloth is of " a red Color; I mean, it's surface is so *disposed*, " as to reflect the *red*, i. e. the *largest*, Rays of " Light. When I say, The Sky is blue; I mean, " it is so *disposed*, as to reflect the *blue*, i. e. the " *smallest*, Rays of Light. And where is the " Delusion here? Does not that *Disposition*, do " not those *Rays*, as really exist, as either the " Cloth, or the Sky? And are they not as *really* " *reflected*, as the Ball in a Tennis Court?"

What, in the Name of Wonder, could induce Mr. W. to make these Concessions? Concessions, which cut the Throat of his own Hypothesis from Ear to Ear! For I appeal to any competent Reader, whether the following Conclusions do not *necessarily* flow from those Premisses?

1. That *Color* is the mere Creature of Sensation: which Sensation is occasion'd (not by any

real Tinge inhærent, either in the Object, or in the Rays of Light; but occasioned) by the "*Disposition*", i. e. by the Texture, or Configuration and Connection, of the *superficial* Particles; and by the "*Largeness*", or "*Smallness*", i. e. by the *Size*, of the "*reflected Rays*". This is all very right, so far as it goes.

2. That "*Redness*" and "*Blueness*" (for Instance) are mere Ideas, resulting from the peculiarly "*disposed Surfaces*" of the reflecting Bodys, and from the *Magnitude*, or *Minuteness*, of the "*Rays*" which those Surfaces either strike back, or refract in various Directions. And what is this, but the very Doctrine, against which Mr. Wesley professedly draws his wooden Sword? For,

3. As to the *real Existence* of Bodys, and their Surfaces, and Rays of Light; it is not quæstion'd by Any, I know of, except by the few Followers of Bp. Berkley: and they are very few indeed. Not three Dozen, I suppose, in the three Kingdoms.

4. It follows, that Mr. Wesley's inconsistent Assertion cannot, even on his own Principles, be true: viz. that "Color is a real, material Thing." No: it is an *ideal* Thing: generated in our Minds by the "*Disposition*" of "*Surfaces*", and by the Reverberation, &c. of "*Rays*."

The

The Methodist goes on. " It is true, that, " when they" [i. e. when irradiated Surfaces] " strike upon my Eye, a particular Sensation " follows in my Soul. But that *Sensation* is not " *Color:* I know no one that calls it so." Nor I neither. The Sensation only gives at first, and repetedly excites afterwards, the *Idea* of Color. For, properly speaking, there is no such Thing as absolute Color, either in the Bodys themselves, or in the Rays which they reflect, or in the Eye, or in the Soul. Yet is the Idea founded on a Complication of Realitys. For both the Bodys, and the Rays, and the Eye, and the Soul, have a positive Existence.

But Mr. Wesley has a dreadfull Peal of Thunder in Reserve: which he thus rattles over the Head of Natural Philosophy. " Take it altogether" [i. e. believe the sensible Qualitys to be *no more than sensible*], " what a Supposition is this! Is it " not enough to make one's Blood run cold? " The great God, the Creator of Heaven and " Earth, the Father of the Spirits of all Flesh, " the God of Truth, has encompassed with False- " hood every Soul that He has made! Has given " up all Mankind to a strong Delusion, to be- " lieve a Lye! Yea, all his Creation is a Lye! " —— You make *God himself*, rather than the " Devil, *the Father of Lyes?*" — Mighty pious, mighty

mighty rhetorical, and mighty philofophical. I fhall leave the horrid Criminality of this indecent Paffage, to the Cognizance of the Adoreable Being it blafphemes: and only obferve, that Mr. Wefley's Heat and Prophanenefs (of which he has, elfewhere, given innumerable Samples) are fuch, that he dares to fcold his Maker, with as little Ceremony, and with as much Scurrility, as an enraged Fifh-woman would be-din the Ears of a 'prentice Wench.

But let me afk: Is God (I tremble even to put the Queftion!) therefore " *The Father of Lyes*", becaufe He has not furnifhed us with Acutenefs of Sight, fufficient to take in the *real* Magnitudes of the Sun and other celeftial Bodys? Or, can He be faid to " *encompafs us with Falfehood*", becaufe we do *not perceive* the annual and diurnal Motions of the Earth? Our *Senfes* tell us (and the far greater Part of Mankind, upon the Credit of their Senfes, live and dye in the Belief) that the Sun is not fo large as a Coach-Wheel; that the Moon is lefs than the Dial of St. Paul's Clock; that the Diameter of the largeft vifible Star is inferior to that of a Tea-Cup; and that the Earth is abfolutely quiefcent, inftead of Conftantly travelling (as in Reality it does) at the rapid Rate of about 60,000 Miles an Hour, exclufively of it's diurnal Rotation round it's own Axis.

Axis. The Illusions of *Color*, *Taste*, and *Smell*, are nothing; when compared with the immense Difference between Appearances and Facts, in these and other Points of so much greater Consequence. And, hence, it becomes the Office of Reason and Science, to rectify, so far as they can, the frequent Mistakes of Sense.

I shall add, to these Remarks, a Sketch of what Mr. Locke has observed, concerning the *Qualitys*, called *sensible*. And I the rather do this with some Extent, because that profound and masterly Genius has cultivated this Part of Science, with a Perspicuity and Solidity, æqual'd, I believe, by few other Writers on the Subject.

" It being manifest, that there are Multitudes
" of Bodys, each whereof are so small, that we
" cannot, by any of our Senses, discover either
" their Bulk, Figure, or Motion, as is evident
" in the Particles of the Air and Water; and
" others, extremely smaller than those, perhaps
" as much smaller than the Particles of Air and
" Water, as the Particles of Air and Water are
" smaller than Pease or Hail-stones: let us sup-
" pose at present, that the different Motions and
" Figures, Bulk and Number, of such Particles,
" affecting the Organs of our Senses, produce in
" us those different Sensations, which we have
" from

"from the Colors and Smells of Bodys. Let us
"suppose, for Example, that a *Violet*, by the
"Impulse of such insensible [i. e. invisible] Parti-
"cles of Matter, of peculiar Figures and Bulks,
"and in different Degrees and Modifications of
"their Motions, causes the *Ideas*, of the *blue*
"*Color* and *sweet Scent* of that Flower, to be pro-
"duced in our Minds. It being no more im-
"possible to conceive, that God should annex
"such Ideas to such Motions, with which they
"have no Similitude; than that He should annex
"the *Idea of Pain* to the *Motion* of a *Piece of Steel*
"dividing our Flesh, with which that Idea hath
"no Resemblance.

"What I have said, concerning *Colors* and
"*Smells*; may be understood also of *Tastes*, and
"*Sounds*, and other sensible Qualitys: which,
"whatever Reality we by Mistake attribute to
"them, are in Truth nothing in the Objects
"themselves, but Powers to produce various
"Sensations in Us; and depend on the Primary
"Qualitys, viz. Bulk, Figure, Texture, and
"Motion of Parts.

"Flame is denominated *hot*, and *bright*:
"Snow, *white*, and *cold*: Manna, *white*, and
"*sweet*: from the Ideas they produce in Us.
"Whoever considers, that the same *Fire*, which,
"at one Distance, produces in us the Sensation
"of

"of *Warmth*, does, at a nearer Approach, pro-
"duce in us the far different Sensation of *Pain*;
"ought to bethink himself, what Reason he has
"to say, that his Idea of *Warmth*, which was
"produced in him by the Fire, is actually *in* the
"Fire; and his Idea of *Pain*, which the same
"Fire produced in him, is *not* in the Fire. Why
"are Whiteness and Cold in Snow, and Pain
"not; when it produces both one and the other
"of those Ideas in us, and can do neither, but
"by the Bulk, Figure, Number, and Motion,
"of it's solid Parts?

"The particular *Bulk*, *Number*, *Figure*, and
"*Motion*, of the Parts of Fire or Snow, *are*
"*really in* those Bodys, whether any one's Senses
"perceive them, or no: and may therefore be
"called *real Qualitys*. But *Light*, *Heat*, *White-*
"*ness*, or *Coldness*, are *no more really in* Snow or
"Fire, than *Sickness* or *Pain is* IN *Manna*. Take
"away the Sensation of them; let not the Eyes
"see Light or Colors, nor the Ears hear Sounds;
"let the Palate not taste, nor the Nose smell;
"and *all Colors, Tastes, Odors, and Sounds*, as
"they are such particular Ideas, *vanish and cease*,
"and are reduced to their Causes, viz. Bulk,
"Figure, and Motions of Parts.

"Let us consider the red and white Colors in
"*Porphyry* [Marble]. Hinder Light but from
"striking

" ſtriking on it, and it's Colors vaniſh: it no
" longer produces any ſuch Ideas in Us. Upon
" the Return of Light, it produces theſe Appear-
" ances again. Can any one think, that any
" *real Alterations* are made in the Porphyry, by
" the Preſence or Abſence of Light; and that
" thoſe Ideas of Whiteneſs and Redneſs are *really*
" *in* Porphyry in the Light, when 'tis plain it
" has *no Color* in the Dark? It has, indeed, ſuch
" a Configuration of Particles, both Night and
" Day, as are *apt*, by the Rays of Light re-
" bounding from ſome Parts of that hard Stone,
" to produce in us the *Idea* of Redneſs, and from
" others the *Idea* of Whiteneſs: but Whiteneſs
" and Redneſs are *not in it*, at any Time; but
" only ſuch a *Texture*, as has Power to produce
" ſuch a Senſation in Us.

" Pound an Almond: and the clear white
" *Color* will be turned into a dirty one; and the
" ſweet *Taſte* into an oily one. What real altera-
" tion can the Beating of a Peſtle make in any
" Body, but an Alteration in the *Texture* of it?

" He that will examine his complex Idea of
" Gold, will find ſeveral of the *Ideas*, that make
" it up, to be only *Powers:* as the Power of be-
" ing melted, but of not ſpending itſelf in the
" Fire; and of being diſſolved in Aqua Regia.
" Which are Ideas, as neceſſary to make up our
" complex

"complex Idea of Gold, as it's Color and
"Weight: which, if duly confider'd, are nothing
"but different Powers. For, to fpeak truly,
"Yellownefs is not actually in Gold, but is a
"Power in Gold to produce that *Idea* in Us, by
"our Eyes, when placed in a due Light. And
"the Heat, which we cannot leave out of our
"*Idea* of the Sun, is no more really in the Sun,
"than is the white Color which it introduces into
"Wax. Thefe are both equally Powers in the
"Sun, operating by the Motion and Figure of
"it's infenfible Parts fo on a Man, as to make
"him have the *Idea* of Heat; and fo on Wax,
"as to make it capable to produce in a Man the
"*Idea* of White.

"Had we Senfes, acute enough to difcern the
"*minute Particles* of Bodys, and the *real Conftitu-*
"*tion* on which their fenfible Qualitys depend;
"I doubt not, but they would produce *quite*
"*different Ideas* in us, and that, which now
"[feems] the Yellow Color of Gold, would then
"difappear, and, in Stead of it, we fhould fee an
"admirable Texture of Parts of a certain Size
"and Figure.

"This *Microfcopes* plainly difcover to us. For
"what, to our naked Eyes, produces [the Sem-
"blance of] a certain Color, is, by thus augment-
"ing the Acutenefs of our Senfes, difcovered
"to

"to be quite a different Thing: and the thus altering, as it were, the Proportion of the Bulk of the Minute Parts of a color'd Object to our usual Sight, produces different Ideas from what it did before.

"Thus *Sand*, or *pounded Glass*, which is opake, and white, to the naked Eye; is pellucid, in a Microscope. And an *Hair*, seen this Way, loses its former Color, and is in a great Measure pellucid, with a Mixture of bright, sparkling Colors, such as appear from the Refraction of Diamonds, and other pellucid Bodys. *Blood*, to the naked Eye, appears all red: but, by a good Microscope, wherein it's lesser Parts appear, shews only some few Globules of Red, swimming in a pellucid Liquor. And how those red Globules would appear, if Glasses could be found, that could magnify them yet 1000, or 10,000 Times more, is uncertain *."

No Dishonor will accrue to this great Man, now so largely quoted; by observing, that, in what he so ably delivered concerning the Secondary or sensible Qualitys of Matter, he stood on the Shoulders of his illustrious Forerunner in Science, Mr. BOYLE.— Permit me, at once, to *enrich* the present Appendix, with a few

* Locke's Essay, Book 2. Chap. 8, and Chap. 23.

Paragraphs

Paragraphs from this laſt-mention'd Philoſopher; and to *confirm* it's general Drift, by the Sanction of ſo exalted an Authority.

"I do not deny, that Bodys may be ſaid, in
"a very favorable Senſe, to have thoſe Qualitys
"[potentially], which we call Senſible, though
"there were no Animals in the World. For a
"Body, in that Caſe, may have ſuch a Diſpo-
"ſition of it's conſtituent Corpuſcles, that, IF it
"were duly applyed to the *Senſory* of an Animal,
"it would produce ſuch a ſenſible [Effect], which
"a Body of another Texture would not. Thus,
"though, if there were no *Animals*, there would
"be no ſuch Thing as *Pain*; yet a [Thorn]
"may, upon account of it's Figure, be fitted to
"cauſe Pain, in Caſe it were moved againſt a
"Man's Finger: whereas a blunt Body, moved
"againſt it with no greater Force, is not fitted
"to cauſe any ſuch Perception. So Snow, tho',
"if there were no lucid Body, nor Organ of Sight,
"in the World, would exhibit no Color at all
"(for I could not find it had any, in Places ex-
"actly darkened); yet hath it a greater *Diſpoſi-*
"*tion*, than a Coal, or Soot, to reflect Store of
"Light outwards, when the Sun ſhines upon
"them all three. We ſay, that a Lute is in
"Tune, whether it be actually played upon or
"no, if the Strings be all ſo duely ſtretched, as
"that

"that it would appear to be in Tune, IF it were played on.

"Thrust a Pin into a Man's Finger, both before and after his Death. Though the Pin be as sharp, at one Time, as at another; and makes, in both Cases alike, a Solution of Continuity; yet, in the former Case, the Action of the Pin will produce Pain: and not in the latter, because, in this, the pricked Body wants the Soul, and, consequently, the perceptive Faculty.—So, if there were no sensitive Beings, those Bodys, which are now the Objects of our Senses, would be no more than *dispositively* endued with Colors, Tastes, and the like: but *actually* with only the more catholic Affections of Bodys, as Figure, Motion, Texture, &c.

"To illustrate this yet a little farther. Suppose a Man should beat a Drum, at some Distance from the Mouth of a Cave, conveniently situated to return the Noise he makes. People will presently conclude, that the Cave has an Echo: and will be apt to fancy, upon that Account, some * real Property in the Place,

"to

---

* REAL PROPERTYS it undoubtedly has: and 'tis impossible that any Portion of Matter should be without them. But Mr. Boyle means, that the particular Effect, which we term *Sound*, is not of the Number of those real Propertys,

but

" to which the Echo is said to belong. Yet, to
" speak physically of Things, this peculiar Qua-
" lity, or Property, which we fancy to be in the
" Cave; is, in It, nothing else but the Hollow-
" ness of it's *Figure*, whereby it is so disposed,
" as, when the Air beats against it, to reflect the
" Motion towards the Place whence that Motion
" began. And what passes on the Occasion, is
" indeed but this: the Drumstick, falling on the
" Drum, makes a Percussion of the Air, and
" puts that fluid Body in an undulating Motion;
" and the aërial Waves, thrusting on one another,
" 'till they arrive at the hollow Superficies of the
" Cave, have, by reason of It's Resistance and
" Figure, their Motion determined the contrary
" Way: namely, backward, towards that Part
" where the Drum was when it was struck. So
" that, in That which here happens, there in-
" tervenes nothing but the *Figure* of one Body,
" and the *Motion* of another: tho' if a Man's
" Ear chance to be in the Way of these Motions
" of the Air forward and backward, it gives him
" a *Perception* of them, which he calls *Sound*.

but merely sensitive and ideal; and becomes so, when Matter, under certain Modes and Circumstances of Figure and Motion, is objected to and operates upon the suitably disposed Organ of a perceiving Animal.

" And

"And whereas one Body doth often seem to produce, in another, divers such Qualitys as we call sensible; which Qualitys therefore seem not to need any Reference to our Senses; I consider, that, when one inanimate Body works upon another, there is nothing really produced by the Agent, in the Patient, save some local *Motion* of its Parts, or some change of *Texture* consequent upon that Motion: but, by means of its Effects upon our Organs of Sense, we are induced to attribute this or that Quality to it. So, if a piece of transparent Ice be, by the falling of some heavy and hard Body upon it, broken into a gross Powder that looks whitish; the falling Body doth nothing to the Ice, but break it into very small Fragments, lying confusedly upon one another: tho', by reason of the Fabric of the World and of our Eyes, there does, in the day-time, upon this Comminution, ensue such a kind of *copious Reflection of the incident Light* to our Eyes, as we call *Whiteness*. And when the Sun, by thawing this broken Ice, destroys it's Whiteness, and makes it become diaphonous, which it was not before; the Sun does no more than *alter the Texture* of the component Parts, by putting them into *Motion*, and, thereby, into a *new Order:* in which, by reason of

"the

" the Difpofition of the intercepting Pores, they
" reflect but few of the incident Beams of Light,
" and tranfmit moft of them.

" When you polifh a rough Piece of Silver,
" that which is really done is but the Depreffion
" of the little protuberant Parts, into one Level
" with the reft of the Superficies: though, upon
" this mechanical Change of the Texture of the
" fuperficial Parts, we Men fay, that it hath loft
" the Quality of Roughnefs, and acquired that of
" Smoothnefs; becaufe, whereas the Exftances
" did, before, by their Figure, refift a little the
" Motion of our Finger, our Finger now meets
" with no fuch offenfive Refiftence.

" Fire will make Wax flow, and enable it to
" burn a Man's Hand. And yet this does not
" argue in it any inhærent Quality of Heat, dif-
" tinct from the POWER it hath of putting the
" fmall Parts of the Wax into fuch a Motion, as
" that their Agitation furmounts their Co-hæfion.
" But tho' we fuppofe the Fire to do no more
" than varioufly and brifkly to *agitate* the infenfi-
" ble Parts of the Wax, That may fuffice to
" make us think the Wax endued with a Quality
" of *Heat*; becaufe, if fuch Agitation be greater
" than That of our Organs of Touch, it pro-
" duces in us the *Senfation* we call Heat: which
" is fo much a Relative to the Senfory which ap-
" pre-

" prehends it, that the same luke-warm Water
" (i. e. Water whose Corpuscles are moderately
" agitated by the Fire) will seem hot to one of a
" Man's Hands, if that Hand be very cold; and
" cold to the other, in Case it be very hot; tho'
" both of 'em be the same Man's Hands.——
" —— Bodys, in a World constituted as our's
" now is, being brought to act upon the most
" curiously contrived Sensorys of Animals, may,
" upon both these Accounts, exhibit many dif-
" ferent sensible Phænomena: which, however
" we look upon them as distinct Qualitys, are
" but the consequent Effects of the often-men-
" tioned *catholic Affections* of Matter, and dedu-
" cible from the *Size, Shape, Motion*, (or *Rest*),
" *Posture, Order*, and the *resulting Texture*, of the
" insensible Parts of Bodys. And therefore,
" though, for Shortness of Speech, I shall not
" scruple to make Use of the Word, QUALITYS,
" since it is already so generally received; yet,
" I would be understood to mean it, in a Sense
" suitable to the Doctrine above delivered *."

But there is one Consideration, which, in my View of it, decides the Quæstion absolutely and irrefragably. To wit, *the essential* SAMENESS *of Matter in* ALL *Bodys whatever.*

* Boyle's *Origin of Forms and Qualitys*, P. 31 — 38. Edit. *Oxf.* 1667.

The Opinion, that what are commonly termed the *four Elements* (viz. Earth, Water, Air, and Fire) are so much *simple* and *essentially different* Principles, or absolute and first Rudiments; seems, to me, an excedingly erroneous Supposition. For I take those *Elements*, as they are usually styled, to be, themselves, but so many *various Modifications* of that *same, simple Matter*, whereof all Body, or extended Substance, without Exception, consists *.

Now,

---

* Without entering either deeply, or extensively, into the Considerations which determine me to this Belief; I would barely offer the following Hints.

1. To imagine, that Infinite Wisdom would *multiply* Essences, *without reasonable Cause*; were to foster an Hypothesis directly contrary to that beautifull *Simplicity*, which, so evidently, and so universally, characterizes the variegated Works of God. Nature (i. e. Omnipotence behind the Curtain) is *radically frugal*, tho' it's Phænomena exhibit almost an Infinity of *modal Diversification*. Two Essences only (viz. Spirit and Matter) are fully sufficient, to account for every Appearance, and to answer every known Purpose, of Creation, and of Providence. What Occasion, then, for *five?* or, as some suppose, for no fewer than *seven*; viz. Earth, Water, Air, Fire, Light, Æther, and Spirit? Might we not, just as rationally, dream of seventy, or even seventy Millions, of Essences?

Sir Isaac Newton's Rule for philosophizing, and the Argument on which he grounds it, strike *me* with all the Force of Self-Evidence: *Causas Rerum naturalium non plures admitti debere, quàm quæ et veræ sint, & earum Phænomenis explicandis*

SUFFICIANT,

Now, if it be allowed, that all Matter is essentially the same, under every possible Diversity of Appearance;

SUFFICIANT. *Dicunt utique Philosophi: Natura nihil agit frustra; & frustra fit, per plura, quod fieri potest per pauciora. Natura enim simplex est, & Rerum Causis superfluis non luxuriat.* If this be just, the Admission of more Essences, than Two, would be totally inconsistent with a first and fundamental Principle of all natural Knowledge.

2. The four Classes of Matter, commonly called *Elements*, are, in reality, not *simple*, but *exceedingly compound*, Bodys; and partake very much of each other. Which Circumstance forms no inconsiderable Branch of that αταξια, or *Confusion*, literally so termed; introduced by Original Sin. Thus,

EARTH associates to itself all the solvable Substances that are committed to it's Bosom. Which Substances, after the Time respectively requisit for their Solution, and for their Co-alescence with the Earth; are not distinguishable from original Earth itself.

WATER is known to comprehend every Species of earthy Particles; as well as to include no small Portion of Air: and to be capable, by Motion, of assuming that Quality which we term Heat; even in such a Degree, as to be no less intolerable by Animals, than Flame itself.

AIR is constantly intermingled with an immense Number of dissimilar Particles. With *houshold Dust* (for Instance), which is, in fact, the Wearings of almost every Thing. Not to mention the countless Effluvia, with which the Atmosphere is charged, incessantly flying off from animal Bodys, both sound and putrescent; and from the whole World of vegetable Substances, both fragrant and fœtid. Those Particles, through the continual Attrition occasioned by their

Motion

Appearance; 'twill follow, that what we call *Sensible Qualitys* are, rather, *modal* Discriminations, than *real* Differences.

Let us apply this Doctrine to *Colors*.

Several Motion and Interference with each other, and by the ambient Pressure of the Air upon them all; undergo, 'tis probable, a gradual atomic Separation: and, when sufficiently comminuted, become, at last, a genuine Part of that aërial Fluid, in which they only floated before. — Could we breathe nothing but pure, unmixed Air; human Health and Life would, probably, extend to an extreme Length.

Fire, or more properly a fiery Substance, will burn (i. e. communicate a Portion of it's own Motion to), and assimilate, all other contacting Bodys, whose corpuscular Co-hæsion is not sufficiently close and firm to resist the subtil Agency of that insinuating Power. But, when it's Force is exhausted (i. e. when the intestin Agitation of it's Parts has forced off all that was volatile; and ceases, in consequence of having no more to do), what remains? A Quantity of Particles, equally capable (for ought that appears to the contrary) of being condensed into Earth, or expanded into Water, or rarefyed into Air. — Which reminds me,

3. Of the *continual* Transmutation *of one modify'd Substance into another*, by the Chemical Process of Nature; sometimes assisted, but oftener quite unassisted, by Art: which literal Metamorphosis seems to be a grand and fundamental Law of this lower World; and, if admitted, furnishes me with an additional Argument for the *sameness* of Matter under all it's vast Variety of Modes and Forms.

We may, for Example, ask, with the Poet:

" Where

Several neceſſary Præ-requiſits muſt concurr, to impreſs my Mind, at firſt, with an Idea of Color. —

" Where is the Duſt, that has not been alive?
The Spade, and Plough, diſturb our Anceſtors.
From human Mould we reap our daily Bread.
   " The *moiſt* of human Frame the Sun exhales:
Winds ſcatter, through the mighty Void, the *dry*:
Earth repoſſeſſes Part of what *ſhe* gave:"

And thus the myſterious Wheel of Nature goes round; the vaſt mechanic Circulation is kept up; and, by a wonderfull, but real, εμπεριχωρησις, well-nigh every Thing (I ſpeak of Matter only) becomes every Thing, in it's Turn.

So thoroughly perſuaded am I, in my own Mind, that all the Atoms, Particles, and larger Portions, of Matter, are primarily and intrinſecally and eſſentially homogeneous; that I make no Doubt, but a *Millſtone* is phyſically capable of being rarefyed into *Light*, and Light phyſically capable of being condenſed into a Millſtone. — By the way, Light is, perhaps, no more than melted Air: and Air is, perhaps, the never-failing Reſervoir, which ſupplys the Sun with Materials for it's Rays. Air is, inconteſtibly, a neceſſary Pabulum of *ſublunary*, and why not of *ſolar*, Fire?

I ſhall conclude this excurſive Note, with a pertinent Paſſage from Mr. Boyle: in which that profound and judicious Naturaliſt informs us, on the Authority of an Experiment made by himſelf, that even *Water* is ultimately convertible into *Oyl*, and into *Fire*.

" Since the various Manner of the Co-alition of ſeveral
" Corpuſcles into one viſible Body, is enough to give them
" a *peculiar Texture*, and thereby fit them to exhibit *divers*
                                                  ſenſible

Color. — 1. There muſt be the Preſence of a viſible Object : — 2. The Surface of that Object muſt

"*ſenſible Qualitys*, and to become a Body, ſometimes of one
" Denomination, and ſometimes of another; it will very
" naturally follow, that, from the various [but Providential]
" Occurſions of thoſe innumerable Swarms of little Bodys
" that are moved to and fro in the World, there will be
" many fitted to ſtick to one another, and ſo compoſe Con-
" cretions: and many (tho' not in the ſelf-ſame Place) dis-
" joined from one another, and agitated apart. And Mul-
" titudes alſo, that will be driven to aſſociate themſelves,
" now with one Body, and preſently with another.

" And if we alſo conſider, on the one Side, that the
" *Sizes* of the ſmall Particles may be very *various*; their
" *Figures* almoſt *innumerable*; and that if a Parcel of Matter
" do but happen to ſtick to one Body, it may give it *a new*
" *Quality*; and, if it adhære to another, or hit againſt ſome
" of it's Parts, it may conſtitute a Body *of another Kind*; or
" if a Parcel of Matter be knock'd off from another, it may,
" barely by That, leave it, and become, itſelf, of another
" Nature than before : If, I ſay, we conſider theſe Things,
" on the one Side; and, on the other Side, that (to uſe
" Lucretius's Compariſon) all the innumerable Multitude
" of Words, which are contained in all the Languages of
" the World, are made of the various Combinations of the
" 24 Letters of the Alphabet; 'twill not be hard to con-
" ceive, that there may be an incomprehenſible variety of
" *Aſſociations* and *Textures* of the minute Parts of Bodys, and
" conſequently a vaſt Multitude of Portions of Matter en-
" dued with Store enough of differing Qualitys, to deſerve
" diſtinct Appellations, tho', for want of Heedfullneſs and

muſt have a certain Diſpoſition, Texture, or Conſtruction, of Parts : — 3. Rays of Light muſt fall towards,

" fit Words, Men have not yet taken ſo much notice of
" their leſs obvious Varietys, as to ſort them as they deſerve,
" and give them diſtinct and proper Names.
   " So that, though I would not ſay, than any Thing can
" *immediately* be made of every Thing; as a Gold Ring, of a
" Wedge of Gold ; or Oyl, or Fire, of Water ; yet ſince Bodys,
" having but ONE COMMON MATTER, can be *differenced*
" but by ACCIDENTS [i. e. by Modes and Circumſtances
" *not eſſential* to their Nature as Parts of Matter at large],
" which ſeem, all of them, to be the Effects and Conſe-
" quents of local Motion : I ſee not, why it ſhould be ab-
" ſurd to think, that (at leaſt among inanimate Bodys), by
" the Intervention of ſome very ſmall *Addition* or *Subtraction*
" of Matter (which yet, in moſt Caſes, will not be needed),
" and of an orderly *Series of Alterations*, diſpoſing, by De-
" grees, the Matter to be tranſmuted, almoſt of any Thing
" may at length be made any Thing.
   " So, tho' Water cannot, *immediately*, be tranſmuted into
" Oyl, and much leſs into Fire ; yet, if you nouriſh cer-
" tain Plants with Water alone, as I have done, 'till they
" have aſſimilated a great Quantity of Water into their own
" Nature, You may, by committing this *tranſmuted Water*
" (which you may diſtinguiſh and ſeparate from that Part of
" the Vegetable you firſt put in) to Diſtillation in conve-
" nient Glaſſes, obtain, beſides other Things, a *true Oyl*,
" and a black *combuſtible Coal* (and conſequently *Fire*) :
" both of which may be *ſo copious*, as to leave no juſt Cauſe
" to ſuſpect, that they could be any thing near afforded by
" any little Spirituous Parts, which may be preſumed to
" have

towards, and be returned from, that Surface: —
4. My Organs of Sight muſt (1.) be of ſuch a *Structure*, and (2.) be in ſo found a *State*, as duly to admit the Impreſſion naturally reſulting from the above Complication of Circumſtances. Who, that conſiders all this, can doubt, a Moment, whether the Idea of Color, with which my Mind is affected, on it's Perception of an Object; depend, as abſolutely, on the Structure and on the State of my Eyes, as on the ſuperficial Diſpoſition and Illumination of the Object itſelf? Yea, it depends *much more* on the former, than on the latter. For, as it has lately been well argued, " If all Mankind had jaundiced Eyes, they muſt " have been under a Neceſſity of concluding, that " every Object was tinged with Yellow: and, " indeed, according to this new Syſtem" [viz. the Syſtem which ſuppoſes that Bodys *are* of the Colors they *ſeem* to be of], " it would then have " *been* ſo; not in Appearance only, but alſo *in* " *Reality!* *"

Beſides: was it to be granted, that ' *Color* is a ' *real, material* Thing'; ſuch Conceſſion would

" have been communicated, by that Part of the Vegetable " that is firſt put into the Water, to that far greater Part of " it which was committed to Diſtillation." *Origin of Forms*, &c. P. 61—63.
  * Dr. *Prieſtley*'s Examination of *Beattie*, &c. P. 143.

naturally engender a farther Mistake, viz. that at least those seven Colors, which are denominated *original* ones, and which *appear* so very different from each other, are in fact so many different Essences. But as this Conclusion, tho' forcibly deducible from the Præmise, would be fraught with Absurditys neither few nor small; we may fairly suspect the Præmise itself to be untrue.

An Objection was lately started, in private Company, against the Doctrine which maintains the universal Sameness of Matter; as if, upon this Hypothesis, it would follow, that " All Bodys, and " all Qualitys of Bodys, are equally estimable." Nothing, however, can be more frivolous than such a Supposition. It might as plausibly be alledged, that, ' Because all Actions, consider'd as ' Actions, are Exertions of Power; therefore, all ' Actions are equally good.' Whereas the *Modes* and *Effects* of Action occasion such vast *relative* Differences in Actions themselves; that a Man of common Understanding and Virtue cannot long hæsitate, what species of Action to approve. Thus it is, with regard to Bodys, and Semblances. For,

" Tho' the same Sun, with all-diffusive Rays,
Blush in the Rose, and in the Diamond blaze;
We prize the stronger Effort of his Pow'r,
And justly set the Gem above the Flow'r."

If

If a philosophic Lady visit a Mercer's Shop, with a View to select the brightest Silk it affords; the Fair Customer will be naturally led to fix her Choice on That, whose Colorings appear, to Her, the most elegant and vivid: tho' she knows that those Colorings are illusive, and that, in reality, there is no such Thing as absolute Color at all.

In short, we are so constituted, as to receive much more delectable Ideas, from some Semblances, and from some Combinations of Semblances, than from Others. And we, with very good Reason, like or dislike accordingly. Though, were our Organs contrarily fabricated to what they are; the same Objects, which now give us Pleasure, would be Sources of Pain: and what we now relish as desireable, and admire as beautifull, would strike us as disgustfull and deformed.

How often are Pleasures and Pains generated by *imaginary* Considerations! And yet those Pains and Pleasures are as *real*, and sometimes *still* MORE *poignant* and exquisit, than if they were justly founded.

Dr. Dodderidge has some concise Observations, on the secondary Qualitys of Body, much to the Purpose of my general Argument. " The same
" external

"external Qualitys, in Objects, may excite dif-
"ferent Ideas in different Persons.

"1. If the *Organs* of Sensation be at all dif-
"ferent, the *Ideas* of the same Object must be
"proportionably so, while the same Laws of
"Nature prevail.

"2. It is probable, there may be some Degree
"of Difference, in the Organs of different Per-
"sons. For Instance: in the Distance of the
"*Retina* and *chrystallin Humor* of the Eye; in
"the Degree of Extension in the *Tympanum* of
"the Ear; in the Acrimony of the *Saliva*; &c.
"And the Variety, which is observable in the
"Faces, the Voices, and the Bones, of Men;
"and almost through the whole face of Nature;
"would lead us to suspect, that the same Variety
"might take place here.

"3. Those Things, which are *very pleasing* to
"One, are *extremely disagreeable* to Another.

"4. Those Things which are, at one Time,
"very agreeable; are, at another, very disa-
"greeable; *to the* SAME *Person:* when the Or-
"gans of his Body are indisposed, or when other
"disagreeable Ideas are associated with those that
"had once been gratefull [*]."

[*] *Dodderidge*'s Lectures, P. 15.

Thus,

Thus, as Mr. Boyle remarks, " Some Men, " whose Appetites are gratified by *decayed Cheese*, " think it then not to have *degenerated*, but to " have attained it's *best State*, when, having lost " it's former Color and Smell and Taste, and, " which is more, being in great Part turned into " those Insects called Mites; 'tis both, in a phi- " losophical Sense, *corrupted*, and, in the Esti- " mation of the generality of Men, grown " *putrid*.*"

'Tis well-known, that some Persons have literally, fainted, not only at the continued Sight of the above-mention'd Viand, whether decayed or sound; but (which evinces the Antipathy to be unaffected) even when the offending Substance has been totally concealed, from the View of the unsuspecting Guest, by those who have purposely tryed the brutal and inhospitable Experiment. — Others will be convulsed, at the Approach of a Cat.—And I have heard of a Gentleman, who would swoon, at the Presence of a Cucumer properly cut and prepared for the Table.

Now, whence is it, that what eminently gratifys the Senses of One Individual, shall thus have a reverse Effect on those of Another? Certainly, not from any Difference in *the Object:* for both

---

* Origin of Forms, &c. P. 59.

the

the Substance and the Attributes of *That* remain præcisely the same, whether the Perceptions, which they occasion in Us, be pleasing, or offensive. Consequently, if one and the *same Object* operate in so *contrary* a Manner on the Sensitive Organs of various People; the Diversity of Effect, where it really obtains, must be owing to a modal Variation in the mechanical Structure of the sensitive Organs themselves.

I consider it, therefore, as equally ungenerous and absurd; when particular Aversions, seem they ever so odd, are hastily blamed and ridiculed. They *may* be, and very frequently *are*, constitutional, and insuperable.

The elegant Sex, especially, are often savagely censured, on these Accounts. If a Lady turn pale, when it thunders; or start from a Spider; or tremble at a Frog; or shriek at the nigh Appearance of a Mouse; I cannot, in common Justice, laughingly exclame, with Dean Swift,

" If chance a Mouse creep in her Sight,
She finely counterfeits a Fright:
So sweetly screams, if it come near her,
It ravishes all Hearts to hear her."

Such Antipathys are not, always, to be classed under the Article of Affectation, nor even of

Præjudice. They frequently arife, more particularly in Females, and in very young Perfons, from the extreme Delicacy of their nervous and organic Syftems.

I fmiled, indeed, on a Lady's once faying to me, *I have juft payed a morning Vifit to Mrs. G———; and really thought I fhould have fainted away, on feeing the Cloth laid for Dinner, at fo fhocking an Hour as One o'Clock.* This, I confefs, ftruck me, at firft, as the Language, not of real, but affumed, Elegance: and I treated it accordingly; by hoping, that, 'in all her future 'Vifits to Mrs. G———, fhe would previoufly arm 'herfelf with a Smelling-bottle, for Fear of 'Confequences'. I will not, however, be too peremptory in denying, that the Sight of a Table-cloth, difplayed at an Hour deemed fo " fhock-" ingly" unfeafonable, might literally excite *fome*, tho' not an infupportable, Degree of painfull Vibration, in the Nerves of fo refined a Perfon.

A few other familiar Illuftrations of our main Point fhall clofe the prefent Difquifition.

We'll imagine a Gentleman to be, as we commonly phrafe it, *violently in Love.* That is: the Charms, or Affemblage of fenfible Qualitys, in a particular Lady, are exactly adapted to ftrike with Rapture a Syftem of Senfes fo fabricated as

his;

his; and, of courſe, to fall in with *his* Ideas of Beauty, Merit, and Accompliſhment. — What is the Conſequence? He becomes her Captive; and can no more *avoid* becoming ſuch, than an Aſpin Leaf can reſiſt the Impulſe of Zephyr. Hence, ſhe is neceſſarily conſider'd, by *him*, as an HELEN, a VENUS, a PANSEBIA.

" Grace is in all her Steps: Heav'n in her Eye:
In ev'ry Geſture, Dignity and Love."

And yet this ſelf-ſame Lady may appear far leſs attracting; or but barely paſſable; or, perhaps, in ſome reſpects, even homely and diſagreeable; to the Eyes of another Man. — Why? Becauſe our *Ideas* depend upon our *Senſes:* and our Senſes depend upon *their own interior Conformation*, for the particular Caſt and Mode of every Perception which is impreſſed upon them from without. Hence, 'tis a common Phraſe, concerning a Man who has never been in Love, that he has *not yet ſeen the* RIGHT *Object*. And nothing can be more philoſophically true.

A Lady, too, may be totally and inextricably captivated. When this is the Caſe, the happy Swain ſhines, in *her* Eſtimation, a NARCISSUS, an ADONIS, a PHOEBUS. Nor are the Virtues of his Mind diſtanced by the Charms of his Perſon.

Other

Other Gentlemen may have their moral Excellencys: but *he*, the incomparable *he*, is

> " More juft, more wife, more learn'd, more
> ev'ry thing."

While, perhaps, a great Part of her Acquaintances fhall unite to wonder, very ferioufly, what fhe could poffibly *fee* in this imaginary Sanspareill; and even lift up their Hands, at her monftrous Indelicacy of Tafte.

PARENTAL AFFECTION, likewife, affords obvious and ftriking Proof of the Theory for which I have been pleading.

> " Where yet was ever found a Mother,
> Who'd give her Booby for another?
> No Child is half fo fair and wife!
> She fees Wit fparkle in it's Eyes."

Very probably. And 'tis alfo poffible, that fhe may be the only Perfon in the World, who is able to difcern any fuch Thing. An Acquaintance, or an occafional Vifitant, fo far from agreeing with the enraptur'd Parent, would, perhaps, cry out, if Politenefs did not prohibit, concerning the *fweet* little Dear, who paffes for the ' *very Image* of his Papa and Mamma';

" Where

"Where are the Father's Mouth and Nose?
And Mother's Eyes, as black as Sloes?
See here a shocking, awkward Creature,
That speaks the Fool in ev'ry Feature!"

Different People see the *same* Things *differently*. And thus, as Mr. Melmoth writes to his Friend; "Tho' we agree in giving the same "Names, to certain visible Appearances; as "Whiteness, for Instance, to Snow: yet it is "by no means Demonstration, that the particu-"lar Body, which affects us with that Sensation, "raises the same præcise Idea in any two Persons "who shall happen to contemplate it together. "I have often heard you mention your youngest "Daughter, as being the exact Counterpart of "her Mother. Now, she does not appear, to "me, to resemble Her, in any single Feature. "To what can this Disagreement in our Judg-"ments, be owing; but to a Difference in the "Structure of our Organs of Sight * ?"

What shall we say of SELF-LOVE? How many noble and delightful Sensible Qualitys does a Man of this Cast *really believe* himself to possess; most, if not all, of which, are absolutely invisible to every other Being!

* Fitz-Osborne's Letters, Vol. 1. Lett. 34.

What

What fine Fingers I have! said a Lady, once, in my hearing:—*How beautifully the Joints are turned!* Undoubtedly, *she* thought so. But Doctors differ. Not only the Articulation of her Fingers, but the Construction of her whole Hand, seemed, to *me,* rather clumsy, than elegant. The same Lady (by the Way) *actually thought* herself SINLESS. But herein, likewise, I could not help dissenting from her Judgement.

A vain *Man* is, generally, still vainer, than the vainest Female. Mr. John Wesley, for Example, declares himself to be " *The greatest* " *Minister in the World.*" I do him the justice to believe, that, in permitting this Declaration to pass the Press, his avowed Vanity was the honest Trumpeter of his Heart. But how few Others will subscribe to his Opinion!—*There is more Learning, in one Hair of my Head,* said the self-enamor'd Paracelsus, *than in all the Universitys together.* Who ever questioned, herein, the Sincerity of that pratling Empiric? But who does not more than question the Reality of those great Qualitys, on which he so extravagantly and so ridiculously valued himself?—When a Bookseller, desirous to præfix an Engraving of Julius Scaliger to one of that Critic's Publications, requested him to sit for a Likeness; Julius modestly answer'd, swer'd, *If the Artist can collect the several Graces of* MASSINISSA, *of* XENOPHON, *and of* PLATO, *he may then be able to give the World some faint Idea of* MY *Person*. — If Scaliger was in Love with his own outward Man, Dr. Richard Bentley was no less so with his own intellectual Improvements. *Mr. Wasse* (said the Doctor, very gravely) *will be the greatest Scholar in England, when I am dead.* — Peter Aretin had a Medal struck, at his own Expence, exhibiting his own Profile; encircled with this humble Inscription: IL DIVINO ARETINO, i. e. *The* DIVINE *Aretin* *. — When I reflect on such Instances of Self-Idolatry, as these; they remind me of Congreve's Observation:

" If Happiness in † Self-Content is plac'd,
The Wise are wretched, and Fools only blest."

We

---

* In setting Mr. *Wesley* at the Head of these self-admiring Gentlemen, I by no means intend to insinuate, that he stands on a Level with the lowest of them, in any one Article; that of *Vanity* and *Conceit*, alone, excepted. Mistake me not, therefore, as tho' I meant to put him, absolutely, into the Company of such Men as Paracelsus, Scaliger, Bentley, and Aretin.

† True Happiness, however, is *not* placed in " *Self-*
" *Content :*" but arises from a comfortable Apprehension of
our

We have taken a Survey of Love, in more ot it's Terminations than One. Let us, for a Moment, advert to it's *Opposite*.

In revolving the Description, which the celebrated Dr. John Ponet, Bp. of Winchester, has given us of his popish Prædecessor in that See; I have been prone to surmize, that the latter *might really* appear as hideously frightfull, in the Eyes of the former, as the following written Picture represents him to have done. " This " Doctor," says Bp. Ponet, speaking of *Stephen Gardiner*, " has a swart Color: hanging Look: " frowning Brows: Eyes, an Inch within his " Head: a Nose, hooked like a Buzzard: Nostrils " like an Horse, ever snuffing into the Wind: a " sparrow Mouth: great Paws, like the Devil's: " Talons on his Feet, like a Gripe [i. e. like a " Gryphon], two Inches longer than natural " Toes; and so tyed to with Sinews, that he " cannot abide to be touched, nor scarce suffer " them to touch the Stones. And Nature, having

our Reconciliation to God by the Blood and Righteousness of His Son. Hence, *a good Man shall be satisfyed* [not *with*, but] FROM *himself*: Prov. xiv. 14. viz. *from within*: or from the inward Testimony of the Holy Spirit, witnessing to his Conscience that he is a Child of God, *Rom.* viii. 16.

" thus

"thus shaped the Form of an old Monster, gave
" him a vengeable Wit, which, at Cambridge,
" by Labor and Diligence, he made a great
" deal worse: and brought up many in that
" Faculty *."—Such was Bp. *Gardiner*, according to Bp. *Ponet*'s View of him. Notwithstanding which, this identical *Gardiner* might seem, in *his own* Eyes, and in the Eyes of Queen Mary and Others of his Friends, a portly, personable Prelate.

To be serious. Let me, by Way of needfull and sincere Apology, for a Disquisition which has extended to an unexpected Length, observe; that, in sifting the Quæstion, it was necessary to recur to first Principles, and to survey the Argument in various Points of View. Let me, moreover, add: that, in all I have deliver'd on the Subject, I do but express *my own* Sense of it, without the least Aim of dictating to Others: or of præsumptuously seeking to obtrude my *philosophic* (any more than my *religious*) Creed, on such Persons as may honor these Pages with Perusal.

Upon the Whole, I conclude, with Mr. Locke *; that " The Infinitely Wise Contriver of Us,

---

* Biogr. Dict. Vol. 5. P. 307.—Article GARDINER.
† Essay on Und. Book 2, Chap. 23.

" and

" and of all Things about us, has fitted our
" Senses, Facultys, and Organs, to the *Con-*
" *veniences* of Life, and to the *Business* we have
" to do. Such a Knowledge as this, which is
" suited to our present Condition, we want not
" Facultys to attain. But, were our Senses
" alter'd, and made much quicker and acuter;
" the Appearances and outward Scheme of
" Things would have quite another Face to us:
" and, I am apt to think, would be inconsistent
" with our Being, or at least Well-being, in this
" Part of the Universe which We inhabit."

F I N I S.

A TABLE

OF THE

TEXTS,

More or less Explaned.

Chap.	Verse	Page.	Chap.	Verse	Page.
			xxiii.	13, 14.	61, 62.
	GENESIS		xxxii.	8.	21.
xlvii.	29.	110.	xxxviii.	10---13.	62, 63.
	EXODUS			PSALMS	
xxi.	31.	110.	xxxix.	4.	112.
			lxvi.	9.	108.
	DEUT.		civ.	29.	117.
xxx.	20.	110.	cxxxix.	13, 16.	108, 109.
			cxlvii.	8, 9, &c.	64.
	1 SAM.				
ii.	6.	111.		PROVERBS	
			xiv.	13.	45.
	JOB		xiv.	14.	203.
iv.	8.	46.	xvi.	1.	64.
v.	12.	58.	xvi.	4.	64, 65.
vii.	1.	111.	xxi.	1.	65.
ix.	12.	58.			
xi.	12.	58, 59, 60.		ECCLES.	
xiv.	20.	111.	iii.	1, 2.	109.
xv.	20, 21.	46.	viii.	8.	112.

ISAIAH

Chap.	Verse	Page.	Chap.	Verse.	Page.
			xvii.	1.	82.
	Isaiah		xxi.	18.	88.
x.	5.	65.	xxii.	22.	88.
x.	15.	66.	xxii.	37.	88.
xv.	24, 26, 27.	66.	xxiv.	26.	88, 89.
xxxviii.	5.	112, 113.			
xlvi.	9, 10, 11.	75, 76.		John	
			iii.	6.	89.
	Jeremiah		iv.	4.	90.
li.	20.	65.	iv.	34.	16.
			v.	25.	90.
	Lam.		vi.	37.	90.
iii.	37.	67.	vi.	44, 45.	91.
			vii.	30.	91.
	Joel		viii.	34, 36.	91.
ii.	25.	67.	viii.	43, 47.	92.
			ix.	4.	92.
	Amos		x.	5, 16, 26, 28,	
iii.	6.	67.			92, 93.
			xiv.	19.	94.
	Zech.		xvii.	1.	94.
xii.	1.	109.	xviii.	11.	94.
			xviii.	31, 32.	95.
	Matthew		xix.	10.	95, 96.
vi.	13.	72.	xix.	33, 36, 37.	96.
vi.	27.	72, 113, 114.			
vi.	34.	72.		Acts	
vii.	25.	73.	ii.	23.	42.
viii.	3.	73.	iv.	28.	42.
x.	29, 30.	38, 115.	xv.	18.	76.
xviii.	7.	82.	xvi.	6, 7.	68.
xxvi.	34.	85.	xvii.	25, 26, 28.	
xxvii.	35.	85.			115, 116.
	Mark			Rom.	
iii.	13.	85.	vii.	14, &c.	68.
xi.	2---6.	78, 79.	viii.	28.	126.
	Luke			1 Cor.	
vi.	48.	73.	iv.	7.	35, 36.
xii.	50.	17.	xi.	19.	10.
					2 Cor.

[208]

Chap.	Verse.	Page.	Chap.	Verse.	Page.
	2 Cor.			James	
iii.	5.	39.	iv.	14, 15,	69.
	Ephes.			1 Pet.	
iv.	19.	46.	ii.	5.	70.
	Coloss.			II Pet.	
i.	17.	28.	iii.	3.	70.
	1 Thess.			1 John	
iii.	3.	69.	iii.	4.	137, 138.
	1 Tim.			Jude	
iv.	2.	46, 47.	Ver. 4.		70.
	Hebrews			Rev.	
i.	3.	28.	i.	18.	117.

INDEX.

INDEX.

A.

ADAM and *Eve*, Necessitarians antecedently to their Fall; 127, 128.
Ἀμαξία, 138.
Ἀταξία, 13.
Ἀνομια, 137.
Antipathys, often founded in Nature; 195—197.
Ἀπηλγηκότες, 46. *Note*.
Aretin, Peter; his extreme Vanity: 202.
Aristotle, his Definition of the Word NECESSARY; 12.
    Supposed Freewill to be the Source of Virtue; 39.
    His Inconsistency; Ibid. *Note*.
Arminianism, supposes it possible that Christ Himself might have sinned and perished everlastingly; 16, *Note*.
    A very unphilosophical Scheme; 29, *Note*. Supposes God and Christ to be immoral Agents; 41.
    Represents Man as an independent Being; 52. 155, 156, 157.
    It's Principles incompatible with the Scripture Doctrine of a future Judgement; 51—53.
    And with Miracles, Prophecys, and Foreknowledge; 73—81. 97, 98.
    Subversive of Divine Providence; 101. 105. 128, 129.
    How far it co-incides with *Manichæism*, 140—143; And how far it improves upon that Heresy, 144.
    Arminianism a System of Atheism; 31, 32. 98. 105, 106. 155, 156, 157.
    The Bane of Morality and Good Works; 158, *Note*.
Arminians, very lame Defenders of Christianity; 54, 55.
    Not fond of St. Paul; 68, 69.
    Are verging fast toward an avow'd Denial of God's Foreknowledge; 97, 98.

Augustin,

[210]

Augustin, St. converted from Manichæism to Christianity; 130, 131.
Αὐθαδισπολια,
Αὐλοκραλογια,   } mere Sounds without Sense;
Αὐλεξασιον,   } 58, 59.

B.

Baxter, Mr. (the Philosopher), quoted; 24, 25, *Note*.
Bentley, Dr. Richard; his high Opinion of himself: 202.
Boyle, Mr. his masterly Observations concerning the Sensible Qualitys; 179—184. 188—191, *Note*. 195.
Brain, fibrous Commotion of, the grand Medium by which an embodied Spirit perceives; 22.
Consequence of its different Dimension in different Men; 34.
Brutes, do not consist of organized Matter only; 35, *Note*.
Divine Providence the Disposer of their Lives and Deaths; 117.

C.

Chance, the mere Creature of Fancy; 122.
If it mean any Thing, it means Uncertainty of Event; 122.
A very comfortless Doctrine; 123.
Charnock, Mr. Stephen, quoted; 86, *Note*. 101, *Note*.
His admirable Treatise on the Divine Attributes; 86, *Note*.
Chrysostom, St. a frequent and favorite saying of his; 123.
Cicero, his Definition of Fortune, or Chance; 12.
Color, not a real Property in Matter; 167, 168. 176. From whence our Idea of it results; 170. 188—191.
Compulsion, distinguishable and different from Certainty of Event; 14.
Conversion, spiritual, an Effect of necessitating Grace; 85, 86, *Note*. 90.

D.

Death of Christ; infallibly Decreed: 17, *Note*. 42. 88. 95.
Death, human, defined; 103 Why the Romans called it *Fatum*; Ibid.
The Act of God's particular Providence; 110—118.
DesCartes, remarkable Anecdote of; 102.
Dodderidge, Dr. his Observations on the sensible Qualitys; 193, 194.

E.

Echo, Theory of; 180, 181.
Edwards, the late Rev. Mr. Jonathan, his masterly Treatise on Free-will; 147, 148, *Note*.

Ειμαρμινη,

Ειμαρμενη, 13. *Note.*
Election, appears to take in a vast Majority of the Human Race; 121, *Note.*
Elements, the Four commonly so called, not essentially different from each other; 185. And 186, 187, *Note.*
Ἡλικια, 72. 114, 115.
ENGLAND, *Church of*; her Doctrine concerning Grace: 40.
   Asserts Mankind to be, not in a State of Arminian Liberty, but TYED and BOUND with the CHAIN of Sin; 106. *Note.*
Holds that God's Providence extends to every Thing without Exception; 154.
Evil, moral and penal, not contravened by the Doctrine of Necessity; 42.
   Are rather negative, than absolutely positive, Ideas; 136—138.
   Voluntarily permitted of God; 129. 139.
   The Divine Motives, to that Permission, unsearchable; 130. 140, 141, *Note.*

F.

Fate, Etymology of the Word; 13, *Note.*
Fore-Knowledge, of God, infers Necessity; 74—81.
   Susceptible neither of Improvement, nor of Mistake; 79, 80.
   Extends to every Thing; 76, *Note.*
Fortune, defined; 12.

Pedigree of, according to the grosser Heathens; 100.
Exploded by the Wiser Antients; *Ibid.* and Pref. vii. viii
Free-Agency, defined; 11.
Perfectly compatible with Necessity; 15—17.

G.

Gardiner, Stephen, the Popish Bishop of Winchester; description of his Person by Bp. Ponet: 203, 204.
Goodness of GOD; moral and praise-worthy, though absolutely necessary: 41.
Grace, internal Operation of, absolutely requisit to all Holiness of Heart and Life; 39, 40. 84, *Note.* 146. 150.

H.

Habitation, every Man's Place of, Divinely decreed and fixed; 116.
Hammond, Dr. quoted; 113, 114.
Happiness, Intellectual; necessarily connected with Virtue: 44.
   In what true Happiness consists; 202, 203, *Note.*
Hart, late Rev. Mr. John, some fine Lines from; 126.
Heat, our Idea of, from whence; 183, 184.
Hervey, late Mr. quoted; 26, *Note,* 60, 61. 120.
חטאת, 138.
Homicide, an Effect of God's secret Will; 110.

I. *Ideas,*

I.

Ideas, not innate; 20. 59—61.
Ideots, not to be confider'd as irrational Beings; 24. *Note.*
Independency, not an human Attribute; 32. 52.
Infidels, their Objections not conquerable by Arminian Reafonings; 54—56.
Intellectual Excellencys, God the Diftributor of them; 35, 36, 37. 61, *Note.*
Judgement-Day, Certainty of, can be maintained only on Neceffitarian Principles; 49—51.

K.

Καυχαομαι, 36.
Κιναυθηριασμενοι, 46, 47. *Note.*

L.

Lambeth Articles; 152, 153.
Le Clerc, Monfieur, remarkable Quotation from; 83, 84, *Note.*
Life, human, it's Duration determined by God's Decree; 110—117.
Locke, Mr. his Defcription of præcipitate Reafoners; 11.
His judicious Theory of the fenfible Qualitys; 173—178.
His juft Remark on the Human Senfes; 205.
Love; Theory of that Paffion: 197, 198.

Luther, his two-fold Diftinction of Neceffity; 14.
Nothing unphilofophical in what he relates concerning Apparitions; 26, *Note.*
His Idea concerning the Neceffity of Grace; 84, *Note.*

M.

Madnefs, metaphyfical Theory of, according to Mr. Baxter, 24, 25. *Note.*
Man, an Animal made up of Matter and Spirit; 18, 19.
Seems to be, naturally, wild and uncivilized; 59, 60. *Note.*
Manichæifm; History, and Out lines, of that Syftem: 131—135.
Enters into the Bafis of Methodifm: 141—143. 145.
Matter, one of the two univerfal Effences; 18. 185, *Note.*
Abfolutely incapable of feeling, or perceiving; 19.
Totally dependent on God; 28, 29.
Has no effective Influence on the Divine Purpofes and Operations; 49, 50.
Is effentially the fame in all Bodys; 185—190, *Note.*
Means, Ufe of, not made void by Neceffity; 72. 89. 113.
Mechanifm: See, ORGANIZATION.

Melmoth,

Melmoth, Mr. his Remark concerning the sensible Qualitys; 200.

Methodism: See, ARMINIANISM, and MANICHÆISM.

Middleton, Dr. Conyers; his allegorical Interpretation, of the Human Fall, consider'd: 141, &c. *Note.*

Miracles, of Christ, supply an Argument in Favor of Necessity; 73, 74.

Misery, inseparable from Vice; 44—47.

Moira, 13. *Note.*

Moor-fields, Bishop of; 33, 34

Morality, defined; 43, *Note.*
Not inconsistent with the most absolute Necessity; 16. 41.

Motives, Intelligent Beings necessarily determined by them; 47, 48, *Note.*

N.

Necessity, defined; 12.
Etymology of the Term; 13.
Distinguished into two Sorts; 14.
Has Place in the Divine Nature; 41.
Most harmoniously consistent with the Morality of Action; *Ibid.*
The Daughter of Prædestination; 54, 55, *Note.*
The Doctrine of the Bible at large; 56—70.
And of Christ in particular, 70—95.
Essential to the Happiness of God; 80, 81, *Note.*
Life and Death entirely governed by it; 106—118.
Not a gloomy System; 119—126.
But the only chearfull Scheme of any; 37. 121—126.
Calculated to impress the Heart with the Love of every Christian and moral Virtue; 124.
The Doctrine of the Church of England; 154.
GOD Himself a necessary Being; 127.
The Christian Necessity does not supersede the Use of rational Means; 72. 89. 113. 146. 150.
Nor make God the Author of Sin; 147—149.
Differs from the Necessity of the antient Heathens; 100.
And from That of the Manichæans; 145.
Arminians themselves forced to make Necessity their ultimate Refuge; 154.
General Remark on the present rapid Progress of Doctrinal Necessity; 158.

O.

Obedience, of CHRIST; at once moral, and meritorious, and praise-worthy, and Necessary: 16. 41.

Objects, external; supply the Soul with all it's Rudiments of Knowledge: 27. 30.

Organization,

[214]

Organization, corporeal; of vast Importance to mental Exertions; 23, 24, *Note*. 33, 34.

Original Sin, could not have taken place without Divine Permission; 129. 139, 140.

The Reasons of that Permission not to be daringly enquired into; 130. 140, 141, *Note*.

To deny that our first Parents fell *necessarily*, is to annihilate the Divinity of the Christian Religion; 130.

Dr. Middleton's Scheme consider'd; 141, 143, *Note*
יוע, 138.

P.

Paracelsus, his Self-Opinion; 201.

Πεπρωμενη, 13, *Note*.

Perfection, Doctrine of, flatly contrary to Scripture; 68. A Branch of Manichæism; 145.

Perseverance, final; a Doctrine strictly philosophical: 29, *Note*.
פשע, 138.

Philosophers, Antient; the Order in which they seem to have consider'd the Chain of Events: 13, 14. *Note*.

Utterly unable to account for the Origin of Evil; 135, 136. 140, *Note*.

Philosophers, some Modern ones, seem to overlook the Agreement of Necessity with Prædestination; 54, 55, *Note*.

The odd Manner, in which Three of them lately reasoned; 145—147. 155, 156.

Pontius Pilate, an Assertor of Free-will; 95. — For which Christ reprimanded him; *Ibid*.

Pope, Mr. quoted; 36. 64. 87. 101, *Note*. 125. 192.

Prædestination, harmonizes with Necessity; 54, 55, *Note*.

Prayer, an appointed Mean to appointed Ends; 113.

Priestley, Dr. quoted; 40, 41, *Note*. 191.

His complete Victory over the Drs. Reid, Beattie, and Oswald; 52, *Note* *.

Prophecy, a Proof of Necessity; 74—81.

Providence, extends to every Thing; 38. 62. 67. 69. 101, *Note*. 117. 123. 154. Necessity another Name for it; 55, *Note*. Particularly concerned in the Births and Deaths of Men; 106—117. And of inferior Animals, 117.

Q.

Qualitys, sensible, of Matter; what they are: 164.

From whence they result; 165. 174, 175. 191. 200.

Would be totally reversed, if our Organs of Perception were oppositely constituted to what they are; 177, 178. 193. 205.
R. *Ramsay*,

R.

Ramsey, Chevalier; collects the Conjectures of the Antients concerning the Rise of Moral Evil: 140, *Note*.
Refinement, social, not natural to Man; 59, 60, *Note*.
Reflection, not a Source of any new Ideas; 20.
Regeneration, not the Effect of human Power; 90. 150.
See, GRACE.
Reprobation: 70. 120, 121, *Note*.
Ridicule, no Test of Truth; 26, 27. *Note*.

S.

Scaliger, Julius; thought himself exquisitly handsome: 201, 202.
Self-Determination; an Attribute inconsistent with the Human State: 18. 28. 52.
 Doctrine of; the very Essence of Atheism: 31, 32. 101. 155, 156.
 Incompatible with a Judgement to come; 51—53.
 Totally antiscriptural; 32. 65, 66.
 Excludes the Foreknowledge of God; 74—77.
 Tallys with Manichæism; 141—143.
 In one Respect, more enormously absurd than the Manichæan Hypothesis; 144.
Self-Love, 200.
Sensation, the only Source of human Ideas; 20, 21.
Senses, defined; 164.
Sometimes mislead us; 172, 173. 177, 178.
Differently constructed in different Persons; 194—200.
Admirably fitted, on the whole, to our present State; 205.
Sin, the Apostle John's Definition of; 137.
Affirmed by Dr. Watts to be a mere Privation; *Ibid*.
Soul, the alone perceiving Principle in Man: 19. 180.
Its vast Dependence on the Body, during their Union; *Ibid*. 21. 23. 33, 34.
Consciousness and Reason two of its inseparable Attributes; 23, *Note*.
Its immediate Origin difficult to ascertain; 109, *Note*.
Probable that all human Souls are endued with equal intellectual Powers; 33.
South, Dr. Robert; his Conversion from Arminianism: 77, *Note*.
Sovereignty, of GOD; 36—38.
Spirit, and *Matter*; the only two Essences in the Universe: 18. 185, *Note*.
Spirits, unembody'd; their Agency the most probable Cause

Cause of human Madness: 24, 25, *Note.*—Their influence on men greater than generally imagined; 26.
Subscription, ecclesiastical, shockingly trifled with; 153.

T.

Τυχη, 100.

U.

Unchangeableness of God, essential to His Immortality; 116.

V.

Vanity, remarkable Instances of; 201, 202.
Vice, necessary, and yet punishable; 44.
Misery its never-failing Attendent; 45—47.
Virtue, does not cease to be such, because necessary; 16. 43.

Indissolubly linked with Happiness; 44, 45. God the sole Inspirer of it; 39, 40. 48.
It's Exertions distinguished into Works *morally*, and *evangelically*, good: 43.
Voluntary, or free, *Agency*; 11.
Absolutely consistent with Necessity; 16.

W.

Watts, Dr. Isaac; his Theory of Sin: 137.
Westminster Assembly of Divines; 150, 151.
Witsius, a fine Remark of his; 109, *Note.*

Y.

Young, the late Dr. Edward, his inconsistent Ideas of human Nature; 59, 60, *Note.*
Fine Passages from; 159, *Note.* 166, 167. 188.

www.ingramcontent.com/pod-product-compliance
Lightning Source LLC
Chambersburg PA
CBHW021844230426
43669CB00008B/1079